WITH A HIGH HEART

BY

Adèle de Leeuw

THE MACMILLAN COMPANY

New York, 1956

PRINTED IN THE UNITED STATES OF AMERICA

This book is dedicated to
Dorothy Van Gorder
with warm appreciation

WITH A HIGH HEART.

CHAPTER ONE

〜〜

CROSSING THE SUN-DAPPLED CAMPUS, ANNE MCLANE
saw the Mouse scurrying down the walk ahead of her.

"Hi!" she called. "Wait a sec!"

The Mouse turned, and when she saw who it was her
face lit with a smile. The girls had dubbed Sophie Whitcomb
that the first year, and the name had clung. She had blos-
somed out a little under their protection and prodding; but
she was *so* mousey, Anne thought with a mixture of vexa-
tion and affection. Dun-colored hair and gray tweeds and
no make-up whatever were bad enough, but her manner
emphasized it She tiptoed down corridors and spoke in a
subdued voice that sounded half-frightened, and she was
apologetic and effacing when she should have been vigorous
and prominent. But she had her endearing points, and the
girls loved her even when they were most impatient with
her.

She adored Anne; her face showed it as Anne came up,
asking, "Where are you bound? You look as if you had a
terribly important appointment."

"Oh, I have," Sophie Whitcomb breathed. "Miss Pruitt,
you know. I'm frightened to death."

"Why should you be? She won't bite. She just *looks* like
a tiger."

Sophie gave a nervous giggle. "You don't mind, I sup-

I

pose, because you're her pet. But she always makes me think she's going to bite a chunk out of me, and I forget everything I ever knew."

Anne laughed and gave Sophie's shoulder a reassuring pat. "Don't let her cow you, Mousey. And all you have to remember today is the name of your library assignment, and the date you're to report."

Today was the day their fates were to be decided. No wonder Mousey was nervous! Anne herself hadn't a qualm. Oh, an excited, happy feeling, of course, but there was not a thing in the world to worry about. It was practically "in the bag." She would be sent to Claremont Library for her summer's work. In between second- and third-year training every would-be graduate of the Library Course had to have a summer's actual experience in a regular library. It was up to Miss Pruitt to scan the requests that came in, and to send each girl to the place she felt would best suit her capabilities.

That was why Anne was so sure about Claremont. Miss Pruitt *did* like her—without going so far as Sophie had done and saying she was her pet—and Claremont was a plum. Her marks were among the highest in the class; Miss Pruitt and Miss Higgins and Professor Dodsworth had all told her she had intelligence and an aptitude for her work. And, moreover, Miss Pruitt knew how terribly she wanted to go to Claremont. It was just about the finest medium-size library in the state. A beautiful white stone building, set in manicured grounds in one of the most attractive residential communities anywhere around; every latest gadget known to library science was in that building—airy and up-to-date and beautifully furnished. Two hundred thousand books, shelved and displayed in the most approved manner; a dream of a staffroom; a chance to put into practice all the things you had learned and to get a new slant on your work besides. And, above all that, the cachet, when you finally applied for a position, of having had your intermediate training at a place like Claremont.

Anne was thinking, as she walked along beside Sophie, that she had plenty of reasons for wanting to be assigned there. Some of them, of course, were purely personal, but there was no harm in that. Claremont was just far enough away from home so that she couldn't possibly commute. She loved her family, but it would be such fun to have a room in Claremont or to share a small apartment with another girl; to be on her own; to have a chance to visit all she liked with Sue Merrill and Beth Paige, who lived there; and to soak in a different atmosphere for a long happy summer!

They came to the gray stone Library Science Building, its windows twined with ivy. A surge of excitement swept over Anne, but she tried to hide it from Sophie.

Sophie looked up, her mouse-brown eyes dark and troubled. "I wish I were like you," she said, on a swift indrawn breath. "I'm just petrified. I hate going to new places and meeting new people—"

Poor Sophie! She knew that she'd probably be sent to some stodgy one-horse place where, because of her very mousiness, she'd be shoved from picayune job to picayune job, and put in a thoroughly horrid summer. If she were Sophie she'd feel miserable, too.

She gave her a loving shove. "Run along—you'll just be in time. Remember now—she's a tiger outside, but she has a heart of gold! See you later, Soph! And good luck!"

Sophie looked mournful and mounted the steps. As she

3

pushed in the big swinging doors she turned. "When's your appointment?" she called down.

"Four-thirty."

"Well," said Sophie, straightening her shoulders, "I know I don't need to wish *you* good luck. But I do."

Funny, Anne thought, she'd never done a thing like that before. It must be awful to be like Sophie—always unsure of yourself, quailing before the untried or the unexpected, going around in a dismal, scurrying fashion, and withdrawing into yourself for fear the world would reach out and catch you in its swift, exciting stream. Somebody ought to push her into it, just the same; force her to sink or swim. It was the kind of treatment she needed, but no one cared enough, or dared, perhaps, to do it. Sophie was a born mouse, and a mouse she would die.

After her last class Anne had a free hour in which to pack. There wasn't much left to do. She flung clothes into her suitcase with happy abandon, her mind racing ahead to the weeks to follow. As soon as she had definite assurance about Claremont, she ought to call up Sue and ask her to look around for something for her. She knew she could stay with the Merrills until she found a suitable place. And even that would be fun—the Merrills were a happy-go-lucky family where there was always something brewing.

At four-thirty she tapped on Miss Pruitt's door and went in, in response to the crisp "Come!"

Miss Pruitt sat with her back to the light—a thin, lithe-looking woman with tawny hair and eyes and a wide mouth. She seemed quite pleased with herself; her resemblance to a tiger was decidedly marked at this moment, and Anne had

4

a foolish impulse to look in the corners for the remains of Sophie.

"You're very prompt," said Miss Pruitt. "Sit down."

Her voice boomed somewhat in the quiet room and Anne grinned to herself, thinking how many students that booming voice had subdued. But it had never intimidated her, and she thought that must be one reason why Miss Pruitt liked her—and showed it.

"Looking forward to your summer?" Miss Pruitt asked, riffling through the papers on her immaculately kept desk.

"Very much," Anne replied.

"That's good. I have a happy surprise for you."

"If she thinks Claremont is going to be a surprise," Anne thought, "she's mistaken. But I'll act surprised, anyhow. And I'll certainly be happy about it."

"Had you made up your mind where you'd like to go?" Miss Pruitt looked up unexpectedly to ask.

The tawny eyes were bright and probing.

"Well . . ." said Anne. She was a little taken aback. What did Miss Pruitt want her to say? "Of course, I suppose we all had a spot picked; but we know it's up to you to assign us, and any place—"

Miss Pruitt said bluntly, "You're going to Kenyon County Library. Know it at all?"

Anne sat frozen in the stiff chair by Miss Pruitt's desk. Her mouth felt stretched; her eyes burned. There was a fierce resentment in her heart. She couldn't trust herself to speak. Surely, surely, she hadn't heard right!

"It's at Tilden, the county seat, of course," Miss Pruitt was saying.

Her eyes swept over Anne's face, reading the injury and resentment written there.

"I . . . know," Anne said at last, forcing her hands to unclench, forcing her mouth to move.

There was some hideous mistake. There must be!

"You don't look pleased," Miss Pruitt commented.

Suddenly Anne flared up. "I don't want to go to a county library!" she cried. "To Kenyon, or any other! I thought—"

Miss Pruitt lifted one long, thin hand. Her eyes were unsmiling. "You thought you were slated for Claremont," she said clearly. "So did half a dozen others, but you perhaps more than any of them. Sophie Whitcomb's going to Claremont, and you're going to Kenyon."

The world whirled around Anne; she wanted to clutch her head to keep that dizzy, sickening feeling from tearing at her. "Sophie!" she echoed. "She'll hate it!"

"It will be the making of her," Miss Pruitt stated. "And you'll like Kenyon, if you'll let yourself. Miss Nichols—Jessica Nichols—is a fine person. You'll learn a great deal under her. And the work is as interesting"—Miss Pruitt paused and fixed Anne with an expression that she could not remember seeing before; it made her feel small and, at the same time, excited—"as interesting," she repeated, "as you make it."

There was no use arguing, of course. You went where you were assigned. It was part of the curriculum. Miss Pruitt knew perfectly well how she had counted on Claremont, and how Sophie dreaded going to a place like that. There was some perverse streak in her nature that made her delight in doing this to two persons . . . as she may have done it

6

to a dozen others. Just because she had the power! She was more than ever like a tiger.

"The library's short of assistants, as practically every library is right now," Miss Pruitt was saying. "You'll have plenty of opportunity to work. I'll expect a good report from you in the fall. And meanwhile—happy days, Anne."

"Don't try to soften the blow," Anne thought angrily. "A fine report . . . happy days . . . interesting work."

She was seething inside.

"I'm disappointed," she said, the color rushing into her face, her eyes stormy. "I'm sure you knew how I'd counted on going to Claremont. And I don't expect to like Kenyon. I'll loathe it!"

Miss Pruitt wasn't fazed by her outburst. "We'll see," she said. "The queerest things happen sometimes!"

She needn't try to be humorous about it, either. That was rubbing it in. Anne listened in stony silence while Miss Pruitt rippled off items about writing at once to Miss Nichols, reporting on May twenty-fifth, and a number of routine details.

"Don't take it so hard," Miss Pruitt advised suddenly. "You're making it very difficult for yourself."

Difficult for herself! *She* was making it difficult. She must be out of her head, Anne decided. Playing mean little jokes like this. *Purposely* putting her in a position where she'd squirm.

She managed to whisper a faint "Thank you" that she hoped didn't sound too ironic, and closed the door after her. Then she leaned against the cool stone wall and closed her eyes.

She wouldn't cry; she wouldn't! That would just give Miss Pruitt additional satisfaction, if she knew about it.

But she didn't think she'd ever borne a more bitter blow. Good-by to Claremont and all her foolish, gay little plans. Good-by to a happy summer. Good-by to everything she'd looked forward to.

Kenyon County Library. It was to laugh! Here she'd been pitying Sophie, who'd probably get stuck with some stodgy, out-of-the-way assignment while she luxuriated at Claremont . . . and now it was she who was going to be stuck in stodginess while Sophie quailed in the magnificent surroundings and the bright atmosphere *she'd* expected to move in. There was no justice in the world . . . certainly none in Miss Pruitt.

"You shouldn't count your chickens, Nan," her father said at dinner next night when she spilled her story into the family's ears. "Much as I hate to sound like an animated proverb—"

"Why wouldn't I have counted them in this case?" Anne demanded furiously. "I had every reason to expect I'd get Claremont. There's no sense behind it, except Miss Pruitt's perverted sense of humor."

"Darling, I wish you wouldn't be so upset," her mother worried. "I'm terribly sorry you're so disappointed, but, after all, *I'm* pleased—it will mean I can have you here all summer. Tilden's just an hour away on the bus."

How could she say that was one of the reasons she hated it? She couldn't; that was all. It made it harder than ever.

"Cheer up, pettie; it can't be too bad, and it's only for the summer. You needn't bother about your room or anything in the morning, and Martha will have nice cool salads and drinks for you each evening, and you can hop into a cold tub. . . . Oh, by the way, Rex called up not an hour ago. He said he'd be over this evening. That ought to make you feel better."

It ought to. Lieutenant Rex Elliott was someone rather special. He'd swum into her life one evening when she went to an officers' dance at Camp Kilmer, and he'd been around ever since. He was in the Special Service division, gay, debonair, very attractive in his uniform, and good fun at all times.

"What's the matter, Mac?" he asked later, taking one look at her face. "The barometer appears to be falling fast, and hardier men than I am would run for cover."

She grinned in spite of herself. "Nothing's the matter."

He scoffed, "Nothing, my eye! I may not have qualified for the Intelligence, but you needn't insult me like that. You look as if you could mow somebody down, and all I can hope is it's not me—I—me?"

"I," she responded automatically, and then laughed.

"So break down and tell all," he took her up happily. "And if there's any mowing to do I'll do it. It might be a good training for overseas."

So she broke down and told him—not all, but most of it. "It probably has a staff of four or five spinsters and it'll be as dull as ditchwater, and I'll die of ennui," she concluded.

"Well," he said, "it's only for the summer. Can't you hang on that long? I'll be around as often as you let me, and between us we ought to be able to dispel the gloom. When does your sentence begin?"

"May twenty-fifth," she answered.

"All right; get your things and let's go dancing. The treatment begins right now. Why you ever went into this

9

business I don't know, but maybe I can change your mind. What's a county library like, anyhow?"

She opened her mouth to reply, but he said swiftly, "On second thought, there are lots of other things I'd rather hear you talk about. Come on. I've got the car and a gallon of gas. And the first one to mention May twenty-fifth tonight is a sissy!"

CHAPTER TWO

THE BUS WAS TEN MINUTES LATE, AND CROWDED TO THE guards when it came. Anne wormed her way toward the back, stumbling over outthrust feet and tin lunch boxes, feeling the thick, smelly air close around her like a blanket. She found an empty strap and clung, swaying and lurching with every motion of the bus as it rattled toward the highway.

"Seat, lady?"

She looked down. A thin, elderly man with sparse graying hair under his striped cap was struggling to rise.

"Oh, thank you; but please don't—"

"I sit all day," he explained. "And, anyhow, I'll be gettin' off at Twin City. You better take it."

She thanked him warmly and sat down. She felt guilty about taking his seat, but she knew that he would have been hurt if she had refused. At Twin City, where one of the big defense plants was located, he got off with a dozen others. He touched his cap and she smiled at him. If she'd had to stand all the way to Tilden—well, she just couldn't!

The bus continued to lose time, and when it pulled in at Courthouse Square it was twenty minutes behind schedule.

"I thought this got in at eight-fifty," she said reproachfully to the driver.

He pushed his hands through his hair and grinned at her. "Timetables don't mean a thing any more," he said. "We gotta conserve tires, and when you go thirty-five where you used to go fifty—figure it out."

That would mean she'd have to take an earlier bus, and they ran only every forty-five minutes. Just another cross to bear, she decided; the summer was going to be full of them. The weather was unseasonably warm for late May, and even this early in the morning there was a leaden quality to the air. Her hair stuck to her neck, her fresh cotton print was mussed from the crowded bus trip, and her newly laundered white gloves had a black streak across the palm where she had clutched the handrail.

Well, she certainly presented an appetizing appearance for her first morning at work! It was all of a piece. She looked around the square with jaundiced eyes. Tilden might be a county seat, but it wasn't very proud of it. The Courthouse loomed imposingly, its glass dome shining hotly in the sun, and a flag hung in dispirited fashion from the flagpole. But radiating from the Square were rows of small shops, windows plastered with advertisements, the sidewalks littered with torn papers and refuse. "Man-power shortage," she knew, would have been the spoken reason. Yet every time she had been through Tilden, she recalled, it had looked just about as unkempt.

There really wasn't time to stand and disapprove of Tilden. She had to find her prison. Normally it would have been housed in the Courthouse, she knew; but Miss Pruitt had said that, because of overcrowding, the Library had had to take over an old house on Cherry Street. Cherry Street. That was a block back of the square. She hurried down the street, turned the corner, and found it—a narrow gray clapboard house with green shutters and a modest sign over the door. "Kenyon County Library, Hours: Mondays through Fridays 9-12, 1-5; Saturdays 9-12."

So this was where she was to spend the summer! In spite of all her resolutions, the memory of Claremont's gleaming white façade with the tall square-paned windows and bronze grilles and close-clipped firs rose before her eyes. She went up the worn stairs and across the sloping porch.

Inside there was a strong smell of fresh paint that made it seem hotter than ever. Beyond the narrow hall a book-lined room opened out, and she could hear voices and the sound of a typewriter stuttering erratically; but a sign at the foot of the stairs caught her eye. "Librarian's Office, Second Floor." She went up the still sticky steps and tapped on the doorjamb.

Jessica Nichols looked up from her desk. She was small, plump, dark-haired, smooth-skinned. She smiled, and her cheek creased into something that would have been a dimple if she had admitted it.

"You must be Anne McLane," she said cordially, getting up and coming around her desk, hand outstretched.

Anne tore off her gloves. "I'm sorry to be late. The bus—"

Miss Nichols said promptly, "Busses have us in their power these days. We have to be glad they run at all. Did you have any trouble finding us?"

"None at all. Though it wasn't quite what I expected—"

Miss Nichols laughed. "That's one of our great charms. . . . The place really grows on you, though. I know it will with you, too."

Anne kept the mask of politeness on her face. Miss

13

Nichols was trying to put the Library's best foot forward; that was understandable.

"But she can't make me like it, if I don't like it," Anne thought. "And it's going to be stodgy, for all its fresh paint."

"Miss Pruitt wrote me such a delightful letter about you!" Miss Nichols was saying. "I think we're very fortunate to have you. We're so short of help that there's a great deal for each of us to do—but I don't want to frighten you. Would you like to come down with me, and I'll show you your locker and introduce you to the girls? Then we can get at the routine little by little. A first day's always somewhat difficult."

Anne kept digesting the first part of that as they went downstairs together. So Miss Pruitt had written a delightful letter about her, had she? Well, perhaps she'd had a change of heart. Or that was her way of salving her conscience— telling Miss Nichols what a splendid student she was! If that was true, Anne thought hotly, why didn't she rate Claremont?

The typewriter stopped and all work was suspended when they came into the big main room. It wasn't big really, and it was very much overcrowded. Anne noticed with disapproval that books sat on top of filing cabinets, and were piled on the floor beside the various desks; the phone was on the window seat, and magazines were stacked nearly to the ceiling in a corner. The workers all looked up at the "new girl." Anne met their regard steadily. She was taking them in as much as they were studying her. At least they were not all the "spinsters" that she had predicted they would be.

Mrs. Bremmer, who asked to be called Gertrude at once,

was well-cushioned and white-haired, with an easygoing manner and a voice that she had continually to keep under control; Helen Grant looked like a high-school girl, in socks and saddle shoes and a page-boy bob, but she had level gray eyes and a humorous quirk to her mouth that told of some experience; and Rilla Andrews, thin, wispy, blond, and languid, eyed her knowingly.

"Even if you only know your alphabet, you'll be welcome," she said drolly. "We're that overworked."

Miss Nichols showed her over the plant, keeping up a running fire of comment. Here was the permanent catalogue; here the catalogue of books out at stations. This was the safe . . . she'd give her the combination later. In here were the books to be mended . . . a frightful lot of them, she said apologetically, but there just wasn't time, with such a depleted staff, to get at more than a few at a time.

"And it's such a pity—because the stations are crying for books, and lots of these are urgently needed." She had tried to get an older woman to come in and mend, but lately she had been skipping half her days because she was waiting for her son to come home from New Guinea and didn't want to be out of the house when he walked in. "That's just a minor problem," Miss Nichols laughed. "But a real one."

These were the regular stacks. This was the way they labeled them; she'd soon get on to their particular system. Here was the table where new books were handled. Could she use the stencil? There was a great deal of that to be done, whenever she had the time. This closet was where they kept supplies. Here was her locker.

"The staffroom?" Anne inquired.

"Oh"—Miss Nichols waved her hand—"call this it, if it

makes you feel better! We've needed every inch of this old building for storing books, so the staffroom has had to be forgotten. There *is* a lavatory there under the stairs . . . but don't gain any weight; there's hardly room to turn around in it, and we're convinced somebody is going to get inextricably wedged there yet!"

Anne spent the morning getting acquainted with her new milieu, and the more she saw of it the less she liked it. Oh, it was pleasant enough—in its way—but everything was so crowded, so makeshift, so inconvenient! It was an ordinary old house turned into a library, and nothing could disguise that fact. Here rules had to be made to suit conditions, and space found where space was available. It wasn't like Library School. It flouted every convention, everything she had learned. It wasn't like the Carnegie at home. It certainly wasn't like Claremont.

She thought of Mousey. Mousey might have been halfway happy here, burrowing in a dark corner of the crammed stackroom, or working over the stencil table, half hidden behind a towering mound of books. Mousey should have been here . . . not she. The injustice of it bit into her.

At noon she asked about a place to eat.

"Oh, I forgot to tell you!" Miss Nichols said. "There's really not a decent spot in town; we've tried them all. So the girls bring their lunches and we all eat together."

Glory, couldn't you even get away from the place at lunch time? It was galling.

"But I didn't bring anything—" Anne said.

"We'll fix you up. I've more than enough sandwiches, and the girls will share their fruit or cookies, or whatever, with you."

Something stiff and hurt inside Anne made her resist the kindness. "I don't want to rob you of your lunches," she said. "Would you mind if I went out and looked around?"

Miss Nichols's shrewd but kindly eyes met hers. "Not at all," she said. "You're entirely free. Just be back at one."

"I've hurt their feelings," Anne thought miserably as she set out down the hot, airless street. "What made me do it?"

But she lifted her head and walked on, searching for a likely-looking restaurant or tearoom. The Henry Lou that she remembered from other days was closed; the Dukomin was far from appetizing, with fly-specked cards in the window and a string curtain drawn across; the diners that proclaimed "Ladies Invited" sent forth clouds of garlic and fried hamburger fumes that turned her stomach. In the end she went into a drugstore; ordered a chocolate malted and a sandwich, disguised in waxed paper, which proved to be dry, unbuttered, with a shriveled slice of paper-thin tongue. She ate it standing up, her eyes on the clock. It was three minutes to one. When she turned in at the Library she felt as if she had a bag of stones inside her.

That evening her family waited for details.

"How was it, dear?" her mother inquired anxiously. "Did you have a good day?"

Anne thought of the stuffy bus and the makeshift lunch, the hours standing in the stacks acquainting herself with the Kenyon County Library stock, and answered with heavy sarcasm, "Wonderful! Simply wonderful! I feel—like nobody's business!"

The rest of the week wasn't much better. She learned to stand at a strategic spot so that she could be first on the bus and have at least a fighting chance for a seat; she learned to bring her own lunch as the rest of them did, and share and exchange; she learned to accept, with as good grace as possible, the little jobs that were constantly being handed her.

"Stencil these when you have a minute, will you, Anne?" . . . "Mind going over these cards? There hasn't been time to collate them yet." . . . "Hand me that *Publisher's Weekly*—it's on top of the safe." . . . "Will you go out in the lean-to and see if *Pito's House* is being mended or in the giveaway pile?"

Being a new girl, she realized that the odd jobs were to be hers. The staff members weren't going out of their way to make her hustle; but it was natural that she should be the one to take care of the little jobs that no one else wanted to tackle, particularly if comfortably seated. She supposed that would be her lot for the summer. In a way her lethargy was so deep that she didn't care. Being unmindful of it was the easiest way; if she let herself get annoyed, she would rankle with the injustice of the whole setup. Miss Nichols was kind, but very busy; the staff members were so busy they could only be casual.

"Get through the summer as best I can," Anne decided, "and then put it behind me. I'm stuck here, and there's no use kicking against the pricks . . . too much."

On Friday the bus was late again. She burst into the Library full of apologies and determined that after this she'd have to get an earlier start, and was met by Rilla.

"Can you drive a car? Answer yes or no, for Pete's sake!"

Anne stopped in her tracks. "What is this—an intelligence test? Yes, if you must know. I drive the family's car whenever I get the chance."

"Then you'll have to do it."

"Do what?"

"Take the Bookmobile out on the circuit. Miss Nichols has fallen downstairs at her home and broken her leg, and you'll have to take her place! She's the only one here who could drive!"

CHAPTER THREE

ANNE SCARCELY HEARD THE LAST PART. "BROKE HER leg?" she echoed in horror. "How did it happen?"

"She was taking down her mother's breakfast tray and missed the top step—they live in one of those old-fashioned houses with long steep stairs—and fell the whole length. It's a wonder she wasn't killed."

"Where is she now—at the hospital?"

"Yes. It's a bad break. They've telephoned for Dr. Cranford; nobody here wants to touch it till he sees the X-rays. She's in great pain, though of course they've given her something for that. The thing is, there won't be any seeing her for some time. We'll have to carry on by ourselves." Rilla gave a shrug. "But how, is another question."

"Oh, I'm terribly sorry," Anne cried with warmth.

She'd known Miss Nichols less than a week, but the friendly, bright personality of the librarian had penetrated Anne's shell of resentment much more than she realized until this moment. She hated to think of Jessica Nichols—who was so vital and quick-moving—immobilized for months, pain-ridden and worried. She was so proud of her Library; she lived for it.

Gertrude Bremmer and Helen Grant came from their lockers.

"Thank goodness, you can drive anyhow," Gertrude said,

with a gusty sigh of relief. "That had us down. We never had asked you . . . and we were in a perfect stew till you came."

"But I don't know the first thing about the circuit, or the stations, or anything!" Anne exclaimed.

It was sweeping over her in an overwhelming flood. A thousand questions—a thousand objections—rose, demanding voice.

"Cheer up," Helen Grant assured her. "We'll tell you all we know, and the rest you'll find out by yourself."

"Well, but—but when would I have to start? Maybe I could bone up a little first."

"Today, this very minute. The truck has to be loaded, and you'll probably be a little late getting places. However, it can't be helped. They can just be glad anybody can come at all."

"Today?" Anne repeated. "You mean I'd have to start right out?"

"Heavens, yes! Didn't you hear Gansville telephoning yesterday? And the Westcott School? Miss Nichols was to have gone Monday, you know; but she stayed here to welcome you, and she made arrangements to go today."

"Don't look so stricken," Rilla said languidly. "I'll go along this time, if that's any consolation. I always have to, anyway. It's too much for one person to handle alone."

Anne forced a smile to her face. "I didn't mean to wilt," she said. "It was just—well, it struck me all of a heap, as they say. What's first?"

"We'll all turn to and load," Gertrude decided. "When we've seen you off, we can settle down here and keep the home fires burning—if any."

"I have the lists and the cards all laid out," Rilla said. She cast her eyes up and down Anne's smart two-piece rose shantung. "Too bad you wore such a niftie. It's hot and dirty work, and there'll be plenty of it. . . . Well," she sighed, "let's get going. I wish I were home right now."

"You back the truck up to the rear door," Gertrude advised, "and we'll cart the books out to you."

Anne went out to the shed that had been converted into a garage, and climbed into the driver's seat of the dark green truck. It had closed sides that opened outward and revealed rows of books, and the back was made of two locking doors that could also be thrown open. When they were open, you could pull out on rails the sliding bookcases that filled the interior. The truck carried seven hundred books. Seven hundred books to be kept track of, carted in and out, rearranged and replaced!

Anne pressed the starter. Nothing happened. She tried again. Still silence.

"Hi!"—a muffled voice reached her—and Gertrude appeared in the dim shed, squeezing between wall and truck. "I forgot to give you the key! This is a tricky engine—it never starts without the ignition being on."

For a guilty moment Anne had hoped the engine might be dead. But with the turn of the key the motor leaped to life. It stuttered a little, refused to die, and she cautiously backed the truck's unfamiliar length out of the narrow shed and up to the back door.

Gertrude and Helen appeared with armloads of books.

"First installment only," Gertrude boomed. "Westcott's one of the largest schools we service, and they sent in a raft of requests this time."

"Gansville wants plenty, too. According to Miss Newton, she's going to have everybody reading—or else!"

Between the three of them, the truck was loaded at last. Anne pushed back her damp hair and went to wash her hands.

"Got everything?" Gertrude was demanding of Rilla as she came out again.

Rilla looked in the box in her hand. "Mending tape, scissors, clips, paste, brush, pins . . . yep. All there."

She snapped the lid and stowed the tin box under the front seat.

It was ten o'clock when they rolled out of the drive. At the corner a shrill whistle stopped them. It was Gertrude. They turned to see her pounding up the pavement, waving two small bundles.

"Your lunches!" she puffed. "Gosh, I'm glad I caught you."

"We'll need them," Rilla prophesied. "And how!" She sounded gloomy, or resigned; Anne couldn't tell which. "And I'm no good without my food." She fumbled in the front compartment. "There's a map here—somewhere—in case you don't know your way. Or do you?"

"To Gansville? Vaguely. We go by Trewin, don't we?"

"You can; but we have Westcott to do first, you know. Carrie Newton can wait; but the school closes at three, and we'll have to work fast to get done."

Anne swung the heavy truck into the highway. "All right. Westcott first. Now while we roll along, and I concentrate on my driving, you tell all. Give me the setup, the low-down, and everything else you can think of."

Rilla was obliging. She talked in a careless, offhand fashion, sometimes lapsing into complete silence.

Anne found the picture incomplete on various counts, but she thought, "I'll have to discover most things for myself, I suppose. Rilla's familiar with everything, and she leaves out the details I'd like to have her put in."

She said suddenly, "Do you enjoy this work, Rilla?"

Rilla gave a lazy laugh. "That's a big word—enjoy. It'll do, I guess."

"How'd you get into it, then?"

"Oh, I had to do something; and library work sounded easy."

"You're not planning to stay in it?"

Rilla rolled her eyes drolly. "Gosh, no! I'm going to get married as soon as Dill gets back from the war."

"Dill?"

"Dilsworth Ames," Rilla said proudly, and with her first show of animation. "Rill and Dill—isn't that funny? I've been engaged to him for two years. He's been abroad for a year and a half. He's a tail gunner. The best in the air corps, if you ask me. He's had two citations already, so maybe I'm not prejudiced after all!"

Anne laughed. "I wouldn't blame you for being prejudiced at that."

Rilla turned in her seat. "How did *you* get up here—sent from school?"

Anne nodded, keeping her eyes straight ahead.

"I thought you hadn't picked it from choice."

There was a dry note in Rilla's voice.

"Why?" Anne asked curiously.

"I wish you could have seen the look on your face that

first day . . . and since." Rilla was frank, if not exactly tactful. "Anybody who ran could read all right."

"I'm sorry," Anne said stiffly. She hadn't meant to be quite *that* open.

"Oh, I don't blame you!" Rilla said generously. "I know how you feel . . . or I could imagine, anyhow. The way *I* feel—wanting to get away, but not knowing how. In my case I have to work to earn money, and it might as well be at this—anyhow, till Dill comes home and we can start housekeeping. And in your case I suppose it was *must*. You just got a tough break on a summer assignment. Where had you wanted to go?"

"Claremont."

Rilla gave a slow whistle. "You *did* set your cap high!"

"Oh, I don't know." Anne was angrily defensive. "I had the marks."

"Well, who got it then?"

"A girl who's going to be acutely miserable there," Anne retorted.

"Just as you are?" Rilla asked. "Oh, wait, we turn here— the school's off this side road. I mean we go this way so we can come in the back drive and park near the basement entrance."

Rilla showed her where to park so that the truck would be in the shade and they would have the least distance to walk.

"Trust me!" she laughed. "I like things easy. Why not?"

In the principal's office Rilla introduced Anne and told about Miss Nichols.

"Too bad—too bad," Mr. Farnham said. He was a small man with thinning hair and a worried manner. "Miss Nichols always knew what to do. I'm afraid you'll find things some-what upset—there's a bit of disorder in the library just now, I'm sorry to say. The teacher who's had charge has been out on sick leave for a month, and the students—well, they've done the best they can, but she was just training the library-council workers, you know, and they may not be quite up to their duties just yet."

"You mean—" Rilla said doubtfully.

"Yes, yes, I'm afraid there will be considerable confusion. But we'll get some of the better ones to help you—I'll call them from their classes at once—and perhaps you will be able to bring order out of chaos." He rubbed his hands over his thinning hair. "I certainly hope so. It looked somewhat helter-skelter when I was there yesterday. I'd hoped to have it more straightened out before you came; but with so many things to look after, and the teacher shortage just now—"

He led the way down the corridors to the room marked "Library." Chaos was a mild word for what greeted their eyes.

"Perhaps you'll be able to get things in order?" Mr. Farnham inquired, without too much hope.

"Perhaps," Rilla said dryly.

"I'll send the pupils along to you at once—at once."

He closed the door hastily behind him.

"He's well out of it," Rilla said. She stood in the center of the room and surveyed the scene. "What's gone on here, I wonder. Basketball practice—or everybody taking what he wanted without a by-your-leave? If we're able to find all our books we'll be lucky. But it's going to take time, sister, plenty of time!"

"It's going to take more than that," Anne said grimly.

The two library-council members burst in.

"Gee," said the boy, whose name proved to be Tim Ware, "this is a break! Are we glad to get out of class—it was algebra! What d'ya want us to do, Miss Rilla?"

"We could start stacking up the books that have to go back," Susan Wilson said helpfully. "That's what we always do."

"You go over them with the cards, Anne," Rilla suggested. "Then if there are any missing—and I suppose there are—we'll instigate a hunt. And I'll do the repairs as they come along, if you'll lay them out here on the table."

Anne flicked through the pile of cards. About three hundred books. That shouldn't take too long. But she reckoned without knowledge. In an hour they had made scant progress. Six books were missing, and a search through the library, in drawers, behind tables, and in all the classrooms failed to unearth them.

"Let's eat," Rilla said finally. "I'm famished. I don't think well before lunch, anyhow. And not so well after," she laughed.

Tim and Susan disappeared with a youthful clatter, promising to be back promptly, and Rilla and Anne set out their sandwiches and cold tea on the big table.

At one Mr. Farnham stuck his head in. "Making any progress?" he asked brightly.

"Not so that you can notice it," Anne replied. "What we seem to need is a detective."

"Dear me!" said Mr. Farnham. "You don't mean there is a book missing?"

27

"There are *six* books missing. They simply elude us. Would you have any ideas?" Anne inquired.

He clapped his brow. "Now that you mention it! Is one of them *Westward Ho*?"

Anne, knowing them all by heart by this time, nodded eagerly.

"The Gregory child has been out with scarlet fever," Mr. Farnham said, "and all books had to be destroyed. The report just came in yesterday. So that solves that!"

He was quite pleased about it, and Anne hated to remind him, "That leaves five."

"But where they can be I haven't the faintest idea, not the faintest," Mr. Farnham said with some firmness. "It's very distressing. I wish you good luck," and he closed the door.

Anne was almost sure she could hear him sighing with relief at his escape.

They worked on stolidly through the early afternoon. Tim and Susan stacked and sorted, riffled through each book to see that there was nothing left between the pages. Anne examined them for repairs that could be made on the spot. Rilla snipped, pasted, put on adhesive and Scotch tape, and laid the irreparables in a separate pile.

"I'll go around and ask the kids in classes if they've got anything at home that wasn't marked down. How about it?" Tim said hopefully.

"Go ahead." Rilla sounded gloomy. "We simply must find those five missing books."

"Gosh, Miss Rilla," Susan cried, "I'm sorry everything's in such a mess. If we'd known you were coming today for sure— But we thought maybe Miss Stewart would be back, and we sort of hated to tackle anything without her."

Anne sent out a call for two husky boys to help her, while Tim was going the rounds, and between them they began to cart out the three hundred books that were to be removed from Westcott, and to cart in the three hundred that were to be left until the fall term and the first trip of the new season.

She was hot and perspiring, and not too jovial. The boys were willing and eager; but they *would* stop and examine books in the Bookmobile, and between loads they engaged in scuffles and arguments and amateur wrestling. It was all so new to her that she wasn't able to cope efficiently with their high spirits and the card catalogue at the same time.

Rilla looked up when she entered with one of her loads. "I feel queer," she said. "Maybe it was one of those sandwiches—I told Mother not to give me fish. Or maybe it's sitting here in the sun. Anyhow, I feel definitely—off." She pushed back her hair. "I don't see how I'm going to finish the afternoon."

Anne gave her a sharp glance. She *did* look queer—pale, with red splotches on her face and a pinched mouth. "Oh, Rilla, you're not going to be sick?"

Rilla said wanly, "I've had ptomaine twice," and, when Anne gasped, "but cheer up; that's not it this time . . . I hope."

"What do you want me to do? Is there anything I can get you?"

Rilla said, with her eyes half closed, "If you could drive me to the Westcott station I could take a train home. It's not far, and I'd last that long."

Rilla lived in Marbury, which was halfway between Westcott and Tilden.

"Of course I could do that," Anne agreed, jumping up. "Is there a train soon?"

Rilla glanced at her watch. "About two forty-five, I think. We could just make it."

They went downstairs together and Anne helped Rilla into the front seat, started the motor, and drove off.

"Are you sure you'll be all right? Would you rather I drove you home?"

"Heavens, no! We can't spare the gas. And you *have* to finish up here." She turned a wan face to Anne. "I hate to do this to you," she said. "But, honestly, the way I feel I wouldn't be of any use to man or beast. All I want to do is curl up in a corner and sleep it off."

"I'll manage," Anne said as brightly as possible.

She felt a little grim just the same. Things were piling up on her, and the fates seemed to be grinning in satisfaction.

She saw Rilla onto the train, watched her find a seat and lean her head against the pane. Then she turned the truck back toward Westcott School, suppressing a mad desire to step on the accelerator and hasten her progress along the winding, dusty road.

School was just out when she returned. She'd have to ask the janitor to let her stay a while longer; for there was a good deal of clearing up still to do, and she had to hurry like mad if she was to get to Gansville this afternoon.

Tim came bounding to meet her. "What d'ya think, Miss Anne? We found 'em—or *I* did!"

"The books?"

"Yep, and where d'ya think?"

"I've thought of every possible place, and they weren't there; so I give up."

"In the trash barrel!" Tim said triumphantly. "I asked ol' Lasher—he's the janitor—if he'd seen any books around lately, and he said he emptied a couple from a wastebasket in one of the rooms and a couple more he found in the broom closet when he was cleanin' it out, so he thought they was meant to be trash and that's where he put 'em."

He led her back to the library and showed her the five books. They were dusty and somewhat the worse for their stay amid the ashes, but otherwise they were intact. Eagerly she checked them against her list, and heaved a gigantic sigh.

"Tim, I'll remember you in my prayers!" she said fervently.

Susan said jealously, "But *I* told him to ask Mr. Lasher."

"I'll remember you too," Anne promised lavishly. "What a load off my mind. Now, young'uns, help me finish up here, will you? You've both been bricks. I'll send you each a lollipop."

They grinned. "That's a promise."

With Herculean effort the truck was loaded at last, the cards in their case, the books-to-be-mended under the seat, a list of Mr. Farnham's last-minute requirements in her bag. She waved to Tim and Susan and set out; a hasty glance at the clock in the foyer had told her that she'd have to do a little road-burning, in spite of the tire situation, if she were ever to get to Gansville in time to unload there.

She took a quick look at the map. Just as she thought— if she avoided the highway and cut across on Number 65 she'd cut off a good third of a triangle. Number 65 was marked "Dirt road, hard-surfaced." That would do nicely, and there wouldn't be any traffic worth mentioning.

She kept a watch for the junction of the highway and 65, nobly passing several drugstores that held out the prospect of a long cooling drink, and swerved into 65 with something like relief. It wouldn't be long now. Miss Newton was probably chewing her nails in impatience, but it couldn't be helped. What had Rilla said about Miss Newton? She'd heard so much that she couldn't remember . . . but there was *something* she was supposed to look out for. Oh well, she'd soon see.

The truck motor hummed and the rolling farmland slipped by in a pleasant blur.

"Someday," Anne thought, "I must really take a look; this is some of the nicest country in the state. And someday, too," she decided, letting her eye flick from speedometer to dashboard, "I must really get acquainted with this outfit."

What was that little knob for? And where did you wind the clock? And how were the lights worked?

Oh, there was some Mertensia! It was almost the bluest she had ever seen. Her mother loved Mertensia, and had bemoaned the gas shortage because she had wanted to go to Peter's Island and gather some for her garden. But here it was, growing by the brook, and an invitation if ever there was one. She'd dig up a few plants . . . it wouldn't take five minutes. She could find a sharp stick, and there was some old paper in the car that she could dampen and wrap around the plants. They'd last till she got home, and her mother would be as delighted as if she had brought her a dozen orchids.

She turned off the motor and hurried across the road to the brook. It was a spot to dally; but she kept her eyes dutifully on the patch of blue, working rapidly and laying her dozen plants in the moist paper.

She looked at her watch. She really *hadn't* been more than five minutes. With a happy sigh she laid the paper under the front seat and pressed the starter.

There was a dull click, and that was all. She tried again, pulled out the choke, gave a series of coaxing little taps on the accelerator. The motor refused to turn over. Her eyes flew to the gas gauge. It said "Three-eighths full"; so that couldn't be it. The motor was dead . . . it wouldn't even whir encouragingly.

She could hardly believe it. She sat there, staring at the wheel under her hands and cocking her head in a listening attitude that, she realized, was as funny as it was useless. There was absolutely no sound, except the sound of the brook near by, which seemed to be gurgling in ghoulish glee, and a cow lowing in a field.

"Well," she said out loud, "this just ties it!"

Now what was there to do? There wasn't a house in sight, though she supposed there must be one around the next bend. That cow belonged to *someone*! She could walk there, and telephone to the nearest garage. But what if the farmhouse didn't have a telephone? It was more than likely. And the nearest garage—wherever that might be, but certainly not on this country road—might not have a man to spare to send to her rescue.

Well, there was no use thinking up gloomy possibilities. The reality was gloomy enough. She took her purse, locked the ignition, and clambered down from the truck. Somehow, now that she was starting to walk, the bend in the road seemed twice as far away.

She had gone only half a dozen steps, however, when there was a clanking noise back of her and she turned to see a farm truck, with pipes dangling from its rear end, pulling up beside her.

A young man with a lean, friendly face called out, "Is that your truck?"

"Yes," Anne answered. "It's stalled."

"What's the matter?"

"I wish I knew!" she said ruefully.

"Want me to see if I can find out?" he volunteered.

"Oh, would you?" Anne wondered if she sounded as relieved as she felt. "I hate to admit it, but a motor's insides are so much Greek to me. I've always said I ought to take ten easy lessons and know what it's all about, but I never have."

He vaulted over the side and walked up to the Bookmobile. His hair, a deep mahogany color, was ruffled by the wind and he wore a sweat shirt, open at the neck, and blue denims.

He lifted the hood and peered inside. "Sure you have enough gas?"

"Sure."

"It could be any of a dozen things," he said reasonably, "but we'll start checking." He worked with assurance, she noted, and he had strong, capable-looking hands. "Maybe the contact points are dirty," he said. "I'll file them a little and see. Do you have a file?"

"Would it be in the tool kit?"

"Could be," he grinned. "Where is it?"

"I don't know," she admitted. "Heavens, I sound like a nitwit—don't I?—but, you see, this is my first trip with this truck. It's all new to me."

"We'll look under the seat," he suggested. "I'd use my own, but I didn't bring it." He lifted out the seat, unearthed the kit and looked inside. "No file . . . a nail file would do, if you have one."

"Yes, I do." Anne hunted through her purse. "Oh, I must have left it in the other bag when I changed over!"

"This was our day for leaving things behind," he laughed. "Tell you what I'll do. I'll give you a tow to the farm— the place is just down the road, though you can't see the house from here—and I'll fix you up when I get the truck to the barn. How about it?"

Anne beamed her gratitude. "I *do* have a towrope," he said. "That's one thing I always carry. Never know when I'll need it—to pull somebody out or get myself pulled out by somebody else." He hitched it expertly. Anne liked to watch him work. "Now," he continued, "you climb back in and steer. I'll go slow. And I'll keep looking back to see that everything's O.K. All set?"

Anne said, "It's awfully good of you to bother. I know you were in a hurry."

"I was hurrying back to do the milking." His grin was pleasant. "Cows don't like to wait. But," he added, "you can't pass a lady in distress."

They negotiated the half mile without any trouble. When they neared the low stone gateposts that marked the entrance to the farm, Anne peered out to catch the name on the mailbox. "Matthew English," it read.

"Well," she thought, "Mr. English, whoever he is, is in

35

luck with his farm hand. He's a likable chap; he seems to enjoy working and he has a conscience about him."

They rolled up the long driveway bordered by tall elms. A low white house with red shutters spread across a green lawn; beyond, Anne could see white outbuildings, a modern chicken house, a big silo, and a gigantic red barn. Everything seemed to be in apple-pie order: orchard trees well trimmed, fields manicured, no old or rusty machinery anywhere in sight.

"And do you know what pleases me most?" Anne demanded when he had stopped the truck and come back to her.

"No, what?"

"The fact that the shutters on the house and the red barn are the same shade! It's wonderful!"

He laughed. "That's Mom's doing. Come in and meet her. You and she can talk while I do my stuff with your car."

"Your mother?" she repeated. "Is this—"

"Sure, this is our farm. What did you think?" He looked at her face. "Oh, I get it! You thought I was the hired man!"

"Well, I—you see—"

His teeth were white in his sun-tanned face. "That's all right. I am. I'm owner, hired man, mechanic, agricultural expert—all rolled in one. Very economical. But it certainly keeps me busy." He helped her out of the car. "I should have introduced myself, I guess. I'm Matt English. And this is Elmway. Mom named it."

"I'm Anne McLane," Anne returned. "Assistant at Kenyon County Library, and on my first trip with the Bookmobile. . . . And look what's happened!"

"I'll do my best to get you rolling again," he promised.

36

He led her up the back steps and into the kitchen—red and white checked curtains, red-trimmed enamel pots, red flowers in the window. "Mom!" he called in a fresh, strong voice. "I've brought you company!"

Mrs. English was sitting in a wheel chair by the bow window in the living room. A thin afghan lay across her knees, from which a white cloth, elaborately embroidered, cascaded to the floor. Patience and suffering had written their story on her thin, sweet face, and her fluffy white hair was knotted low on her neck.

"Come in, dear. I heard you drive up."

Matthew introduced them and sketched in the picture in a few words. He drew up a chair for Anne. "You two can chin while I do a little hocus-pocus. Wish me luck."

"Bring two glasses and the pitcher that's in the icebox first, Matt, please," his mother said. "And the cake that's in the lean-to."

"Only two glasses?" he turned to ask. "What about me?"

His mother said calmly, "If I know you, you'll take care of yourself on the way out."

Anne leaned across to finger the fine damask; flowers, leaves, and vines were laid in an intricate pattern of incredibly small stitches around the central oblong and the border. "It's simply beautiful," she cried. "Is it your work?"

Mrs. English nodded. "Perhaps it seems wicked to work on banquet cloths at a time like this. But I want something to occupy me, and it brings in such—welcome money. I do my Red Cross knitting at night when I can't see to embroider so well."

"It's the sort of thing you only see in wonderful specialty shops—terribly expensive places."

"Those are the people I do them for. I love to use my hands, and it's nice to be paid for it. I have a little game. When I look around at the new rug, for instance, I say, 'That's the dinner cloth for Franklins'.' And the refrigerator is the monogrammed sheets for Peperingtons'. And the wing chair is the handmade underwear for Graves'. And when I want something very badly I say, 'I wonder what *that's* going to come from.' "

The frosty drink was delicious, the cake as light as a feather. "You don't do all your housework, too, do you?" Anne asked.

"No, a woman who lives down the road comes in to clean and get dinner for us. Matt and I manage the rest. I'm really quite good at getting about in my wheel chair. At first I thought I'd never manage, but you learn everything in time. I made up my mind to learn because I didn't want to handicap Matt any more than I had to. He has enough on his shoulders, running this farm."

"It looks as if at least three men worked it," Anne said warmly.

"Matt goes at everything scientifically. He's made the place over. You should have seen it before. Matt's father was a fine man, but he had old-fashioned ideas. He wasn't one to try new ways." She smiled a little, as if she were remembering things. "But you mustn't let me run on like this. Tell me about your own work. I know you do something—all girls do these days. I'd love to hear about it."

It was easy to talk to Mrs. English. She might be tied to her chair; but her mind was not confined, and her interest was all-encompassing. She nodded her head and made little sympathetic noises as Anne talked. And Anne had no idea

38

how much she had talked until she looked up and saw Matt standing in the doorway. His face was unsmiling and he looked years older . . . stern.

"All fixed?" she broke off to ask.

"It's going again," he answered. "It *was* the contact points. But I'd advise you to take it to a garage when you have a chance and see if they need changing."

"I don't know how to thank you." Anne rose and took up her bag. Her eyes fell on the kitchen clock. "Four-thirty! Good grief, I had no idea it was that late! I'll never make it to Gansville."

"I hurried as much as I could. It was slow work."

"Oh, I didn't mean that!" Anne assured him. "But by the time I get there it will be five, and the station closes then. I wonder—would you let me telephone Miss Newton? I'll have to explain. It's one thing after another today. The pixies must be on my trail."

Miss Newton's voice came, thin and querulous, over the wire. "I don't see why you couldn't have let me know before! Here I've been expecting you all day—"

"I'm sorry," Anne said stiffly. She was afraid she didn't sound it. "I was held up at Westcott, you see—"

"Miss Nichols said she'd be out today, and she's always on time."

"But Miss Nichols couldn't come," Anne explained again. "She's broken her leg. And I—"

"Who are *you?*"

"I'm the new assistant and I'm taking her place—on the circuit," she added hastily, lest Miss Newton get a wrong idea. "I was trying to get to Gansville and I had a break-down. That is, the car stopped."

"Hm," said Miss Newton, and even over the phone it sounded sniffy. "Miss Nichols never had a breakdown. Never. She was always on time. I could count on her like a clock. It's very upsetting. Here I've waited all day, and had everything ready, and there were some things I wanted to talk over with you—I mean, of course, with Miss Nichols. When will she be out?"

"She won't be out of the hospital for months," Anne said wearily. "I'm coming in her stead. I could come tomorrow if you want me. I have your books on the truck now."

"Tomorrow's a very busy day, and we're only open till noon. No, I don't think you'd better come tomorrow."

"What day would be convenient, then?" Anne pressed.

"Well—it's hard to say, now that you didn't come when you were expected. Perhaps you'd better come tomorrow anyhow, and get it over with. Though how I'll manage to look after my people and you, too, I don't know. I really don't."

Anne said quickly, "I'll be there tomorrow about ten."

Miss Newton said, with a last despairing sigh, "It's very upsetting," and Anne hung up, her cheeks pink and her eyes snapping.

"How to make friends and influence people! She's probably run the place on her own lines so long she can't bear a rift in the schedule."

Anne thanked Mrs. English for her hospitality, and Mrs. English pressed her hand.

"Stop in again, my dear, when you go by this way. I'd love to have you. My days are—well, I won't say lonesome; but I don't see many people."

Matt came and stood beside Anne as she got into the car.

"You're not keen about your work, are you?" he asked with startling abruptness.

She turned, indignant. "Of course I am! Why would I ever have gone into library work if I weren't keen about it?"

"But this angle of it?" he persisted.

"Well . . ." she admitted, somewhat against her will. His steady regard made her slightly uncomfortable. "It hasn't been what I expected; that's certain."

"Lots of things in life aren't. If you make up your mind ahead of time too much, you miss a lot. But if you go at it with a high heart, ready to enjoy whatever comes—"

"Really!" Anne said, her color high. "Is this a lecture?"

"No," he returned imperturbably, "just a tip. I heard you talking to Mother. You had your heart set on something and it didn't happen, and what *did* happen is so far down the list that you can't even see it. You're on the wrong track, if you don't mind my saying so."

"I'm afraid I do mind your saying so. Your mother at least listened without giving me a sermon—*or* a tip," she added pointedly.

"Mother's politer than I am, I guess," he returned. "Don't get huffy. You could have a lot of fun this summer if you kept your eyes open—and your heart."

"Thank you," she said. "I'm sure I'll get through. After all, it *is* only for the summer." She threw out the clutch and went into gear. The gears rasped noisily, and she bit her lip. "I really am grateful for your help," she said, leaning out to back down the drive. "If not for your advice."

He waved. "Don't mention it," he called.

She couldn't see his face clearly by that time, but she had the uncomfortable sensation that he was laughing.

Once on the road, she pressed her foot down savagely. What a day! It was a relief to her feelings to have the car leaping under her. Here at least was something she could control. But even that satisfaction was short-lived. Tires . . . gas . . . she had no right to go at this speed, no matter how it soothed her wounded pride.

He'd been insufferable. What made him believe he could talk to her that way? He had no right to think that of her. But if he did think it, he might have kept it to himself. Some people always seemed to set themselves up as critics of others, and apparently he was one of them. Well, she didn't need to let it bother her. She'd never see him again. It was queer how, when she said that to herself, she had a little pang of regret. She had liked him . . . at first. And his mother. She would have liked to stop in occasionally and visit with Mrs. English. But now, of course, that was out of the question.

It was five-thirty when she got back to Tilden and to a garage.

"Better leave it here overnight, and I'll see to it early in the morning," the man told her.

She wondered if it were all right to do this. But, after all, what else was there to do? She couldn't risk another breakdown on a country road . . . and another rescue by some outspoken young farmer. She supposed she hadn't seemed very grateful to him. She had had a nice little speech all ready, for she had really been extremely thankful for his assistance. Only, when he spoke to her like that, it had evaporated in her anger.

She locked the sides and back of the Bookmobile and went to the Library. It was closed. She *had* thought somebody would wait for her. But why should they, she reflected bitterly. What did it matter to them whether she was stuck on the road or not? Maybe she should have telephoned them, too. Even so, wouldn't you have thought somebody would have been anxious enough about her to wait a little beyond closing time to see if she turned up or if she needed help? For all they cared, she might still be out on 65.

That left her with the book cards she had taken out of the truck to restore to their proper place in the Library. She had no key; so she'd have to take them home with her and bring them back in the morning.

It was too late for the ten-of-six bus. She stood on the corner a while and then went in and had a coke. While she was there she telephoned her family. They, at least, would care where she was.

"Oh dear!" her mother cried. "What a pity! Rex called up just half an hour ago and wanted you to go somewhere with him. He said something about your having a date with him."

"Glory!" Anne breathed, clapping a hand over her mouth.

It was true. They were to have had dinner together, and then go to the Camp Kilmer band concert. She had forgotten all about it till this moment.

"He seemed quite put out," her mother said.

No wonder! And it wouldn't help matters any if she told him she'd forgotten the date completely. This would take a little fixing. She went out and stared moodily up Tilden's dreary main street, where no bus was in sight. It was then that she thought of the Mertensia, wilting in the car, and the garage closed for the night. She scuffed impatiently at the curb. The end of a simply perfect day!

43

CHAPTER FOUR

~~~

ANNE PUSHED BACK THE HAIR FROM HER DAMP FORE-
head. "Miss Newton, I don't see *Baby Island*. I've looked
everywhere."

Carrie Newton glanced up brightly. "Oh, yes! I forgot
to tell you. I let it go out this morning, before you came;
but I just didn't take the card from the 'Returns.' I thought
I'd surely remember. I *may* hold that over till next time,
mayn't I? I'm sure Miss Nichols wouldn't mind."

It had almost come to be a refrain. "Miss Nichols would"
. . . "Miss Nichols wouldn't" . . . "Miss Nichols always
did" . . . Anne felt that her smile was a little tart.

She stifled the thought of how many precious minutes she
had spent looking for the book and said, "Why, of course
you may keep it. I just wish you had told me before."

"Oh dear, I didn't know you were looking for *that*! You
see, I'm so busy on Saturday mornings . . . Now, if you'd
come yesterday as you planned—as I *hoped* you would—
I'd have had so much more time to help you. And," she
added triumphantly, "the book would have been in! Because,
you see, the person who wanted it didn't come in till this
morning!"

They had been over it before. Miss Newton was convinced that Anne could have made it if she had wanted to,
and Anne had given up trying to break down Miss Newton's

prejudice. It didn't make for exactly friendly relations, but each was being ultra-polite.

Anne sat down at a table in the far room, her lips a little thinned, and set about straightening out the records. It was an interesting place, this little old house that had been turned into the Gansville Community Library. Low ceilings, white-washed walls, many-paned windows, and a narrow staircase winding perilously to a second floor which was not yet in use.

"But we're going to open it soon," Miss Newton told her proudly. "Oh, it will be lovely! As soon as we get some money, we're going to make it into a community hall— where we can have lectures and concerts, you know. Of course it won't be large, but it'll be—cozy. What's that word you read—*inteem*, that's it. *Inteem!* I do think French makes things sound so elegant!"

Miss Newton kept calling to her. . . .

"Did you bring a copy of *One World*?"

"Yes, I have it . . . in the truck." She went back to her counting.

"Oh, and that book by Sumner Welles? I can't think of the title."

"I brought it. . . . Seventy-eight, seventy-nine—"

"What did you say?"

"I said I brought it!" Anne raised her voice.

"Yes, I know. But after that. It sounded as if you were counting."

"I was," said Anne a little grimly, and began over again.

She heard people coming and going, Miss Newton's sprightly chatter a sort of running accompaniment. "Yes, so unseasonable, isn't it? . . . How *is* little Brenda? Oh,

45

lovely, lovely! . . . Now if you want a really good romance —though, of course, I don't think they're what they used to be at all; so many that should never have been written, but, of course, you can't suit all tastes—I'd say you ought to take—"

In a lull Anne called out, "Miss Newton, what does this mean on the card for *Whiteoaks of Jalna*? There are initials written in: H. F. M."

"H. F. M.?" Miss Newton repeated in a puzzled voice. "Dear me! Is it before or after the title?"

"After," Anne said, wondering what difference it could make.

"Oh, after the title! Well, that's 'Hold for Maybelle,' " Miss Newton said with relief. "Now if it had been before—"

"But what does it mean?"

"Why," said Miss Newton, "just what it says. 'Hold for Maybelle.' She said she wanted it when next it came in. So I put that on the card in case I should forget. Now when I look at the card, of course, I see that I mustn't let it go out before Maybelle has a chance to take it; that is, if she comes in within a day or two. I wouldn't *dream* of holding it longer."

Shades of Miss Pruitt! Shades of Miss Higgins and Professor Dodsworth. What would they make of this?

"It's a system of my own," Miss Newton volunteered, not without a note of pride. "After all, I have to have some way of keeping track of things; so I just invented my own letters. It's very convenient. Sometimes I forget, but if I think long enough I can always get it back. I know everybody who comes to the Library; so if it shouldn't be Maybelle it could be Miranda Hawkes or Minnie Deakin, you see, or maybe Mildred Lyons."

"It's a little—" Anne bit her tongue. She was going to say "startling," but amended it to "unorthodox." "It's a little unorthodox."

"Oh, I don't know," Miss Newton said. "Systems have to be invented by somebody, and I might as well have my own."

"What happens if someone else comes in to take charge, though?" Anne asked.

"Nobody does!" Miss Newton said triumphantly. "I've never missed a day since the Library opened. So I don't have to worry about that. And Miss Nichols knows all about it, so I naturally thought *you* would."

Anne was beginning to have new admiration for Miss Nichols and the problems of the circuit.

There were other strange markings. B. L., she discovered, meant "Binding Loose," and G. O. B. S. A. was deciphered to mean "Get Others by Same Author."

"I always erase my marks, though, before the cards go back," Miss Newton explained. "So I don't see that it does any harm, and it *does* help me so much."

Not all ways of running a library, Anne thought wryly, were learned at Library School. Miss Newton had a "system" all her own.

"Don't you ever get mixed up?" Anne couldn't help asking.

"Oh, once in a while," Miss Newton confessed. "But anybody would. And I always get it straightened out again."

Anne bent to her work, a little smile playing around her mouth. She wagered that if Miss Newton *did* get mixed

47

up she'd invent a system of untangling herself. When she came to A. F. M. P. and riffled through the book, she felt as if she had discovered the answer to the sixty-four-dollar question; for it must surely mean "Ask for Missing Page." Maybe, after all, Miss Newton had something there.

"Just as long as she sticks to English," Anne muttered to herself, "I may be able to follow."

She lifted her head a moment to listen. She was conscious that a conversation had been going on for quite a few minutes. . . . Miss Newton's voice, and a child's.

"You had it out eight extra days, Mary dear; so that will be sixteen cents."

An appalled silence.

"You mean," Mary cried, "that I mutht pay thixteen thents?"

"I'm afraid so. Two cents a day, dear."

"But I haven't got thixteen thents!" A quaver in the child's voice. "And I would have come thooner, only Mother wath thick and I had to thtay home. So I read the book over again . . . 'cause I couldn't come to get a new one."

Anne peered around the edge of the doorway. She was a diminutive child with large dark eyes and a dark bang falling over her rounded forehead. She wore a stricken look and she was clutching the book to her stomach.

"If I can't pay the thixteen thents," she implored, "can't I have another book?"

Miss Newton was visibly melting. "I'll tell you what we'll do, Mary. See those magazines over there?" The child nodded. "If you straighten them into neat piles for me, you can have another book."

"But I can't pay the thixteen thents!"

"Never mind that. Straightening the magazines will be worth sixteen cents to me."

While Mary went about her task with an absorbed and radiant air, Miss Newton dipped into her change purse.

She dropped a dime and six pennies in the "Fines" box. "Now," she said out loud, "that makes things right."

Anne went back to her work. She had a new insight into Miss Newton. Perhaps she had her own, highly original, way of running a library, but it was effective. It was human, and kind. Rules were not for her—only the needs of her readers.

In a little while Mary went out, carrying *The Cat and the Kitten*; her eyes glowed. "I'll bring it back right away, as thoon as I read it," she promised. "And I'll help you fix up your Liberry, too."

Anne wondered how often this sort of thing happened. Often enough, she imagined, to make a little dent in the contents of that worn purse. But she dared not ask.

She was staggering into the Library with a load of books from the truck when a voice hailed her.

"Need any help?" It was Matt English. Without waiting for her answer he lifted the load neatly into his own arms. "I see the truck's working today—and so are you."

"Thanks," she said. "For carrying the books, I mean. Was that supposed to be a crack?"

"Not unless you want to take it that way. . . . Where do you want these?"

"In here," she said, leading the way.

"Hello there, Miss Carrie!" he said.

Miss Newton's face lit up with welcome. "Oh, Matthew, how nice to see you! Miss McLane, this is Mr. English—"

"We've met," she said.

"Dear me! You have! Why, I'd no idea—"

Matthew said with a sober face, "Miss McLane was enjoying herself so much at our house yesterday that she decided not to come to Gansville. She telephoned you from there."

"Why—why—"

Miss Newton stared from one to the other. Her expression was shocked, not to say horrified.

"Mr. English has missed his calling," Anne said. "He ought to be writing fiction."

"You mean—he's making it up?" Miss Newton inquired incredulously. "Why, Matthew, I never knew you to do a thing like that before!"

"I was never tempted before, either," he stated easily.

"What does he *mean*?" Miss Newton appealed to Anne.

"Perhaps he can explain," Anne said primly. "I've a lot of work still to do."

She went back into the far room and flounced into a chair. That was a nice thing to do! Putting her in an unfavorable light with Miss Newton. Matters were bad enough as they were. And then laughing at her! Oh well, she'd try not to think about it. He'd soon be gone.

She heard Miss Newton calling, and reluctantly got up and returned to the front desk. "Matthew's come for a special book," Miss Newton said. "I told him it was such a good thing he'd managed to get in this morning, because now I can give you the title and you can see if you can get it for him. It's—oh dear, what did you say it was, Matthew?"

"*Beneficent Soil Bacteria and the Theory of Plant En-*

zymes," he said promptly. "I've been wanting that for some time. Do you think you could get it for me?"

"Of course we haven't it at Kenyon, but I'll write to the State Library at Trenton for it," she said. "And I'll let Miss Newton know as soon as I hear."

"Imagine anybody reading a book like that—and understanding it!" Miss Newton exclaimed. "People do things differently these days. My father had a farm; but he never read a book about it, I'm sure."

"Perhaps he knew things naturally that I have to get out of books," Matthew said.

Anne looked at him quickly. That was a gracious thing to say. She saw Miss Newton beam.

"How nice, Matthew! But of course it's not true. My father—and I'm not saying anything against him; he was a fine man, and he led a busy life and he probably wouldn't have had time to read a book if he'd wanted to—but he just let the farm go along as it was from year to year. And you want to make yours better and better. That's why I do so admire you!"

Matthew English grinned and patted Miss Newton's shoulder. "Whenever I need a tonic, I come over here to Gansville. Miss Newton knows how to make people feel as if they amounted to something—important."

"Oh, Matthew, nonsense!" But Anne saw that Miss Newton was flushing with pleasure. "It's just that I'm so interested in everybody. And I like to see them succeed. . . . My," she said, "I wish somehow I could have the kind of library that had everything in it that people wanted—even books like the one you just asked for! It would be marvelous!"

Anne thought Matthew would go after he had left his request, but he was still around, gazing at the bookshelves, when she was ready to leave. He helped her carry out the books that were to be returned to Kenyon, and stored them expertly along the shelves. He waited while she slid the shelves into place and locked the sides and stowed her paraphernalia.

She made up her mind suddenly and looked at him before her courage departed. "I know just what's in your mind," she said.

"Do you?" He sounded surprised. "What?"

"You were thinking it was a good thing I got over to Gansville and met Miss Newton so early in the game," she said, with a little rush. "So I could see an example of being in love with your work."

"Well!" he cried. "Good for you! That's exactly what I *was* thinking."

"Maybe you'd be interested to know, then"—her voice had spirit in it—"that I'd reached that conclusion myself just before you came."

"Better and better!" His tone was bantering, but pleasant. "I'll be running along. Thanks for seeing to that book."

"If you'd told me yesterday when I was at your house it would have saved you a trip to Gansville."

"But if I'd told you yesterday I wouldn't have seen you today," he returned reasonably.

And, before she had quite digested that, he was gone, with a wave of his lean brown arm.

Rilla was still out with her attack of indigestion when Anne reported for work Monday. She found the Cornell

School on her schedule and set out to cope with it alone. Remembering the day at Westcott, her heart sank.

Gertrude Bremmer reassured her. "This won't be so bad," she said. "It's only a small place—a country school, really, and the kids love to help."

It was set back from the road in a small wooded grove. A flagpole rose from a bare playground in front, and the doors were open from the old-fashioned porch that led into the four classrooms. There were only two teachers, and both of them were in a dither.

"Do excuse the sad faces of the children," Miss Prendergast begged her. "This is the day of the annual play, you know—"

"And now we can't have it!" one of the little girls, who was trailing her, put in. " 'Cause Hester Lincoln—she was to be the aunt—had to stay home 'cause her mother's having a new baby! And now I can't be in the play, either, and I had a new dress and everything!"

"It's a real tragedy," Miss Prendergast said, with a sympathetic smile. "As you can see. The children worked so hard on it, and even did the scenery. You must let me show you what they've done."

"We were going to go on a picnic afterward," the disappointed actress explained. "And everybody had a special lunch."

"Well, Janice, we can still go on the picnic," Miss Prendergast said. "As soon as we've helped Miss McLane with the books."

"I'm afraid we'll have to do most of the helping," the other teacher, Miss Baker, said ruefully. "The children's minds are definitely not on the library this morning. It really *is* a shame."

"Can't some other pupil take the part?" Anne inquired.

"If we'd only *known*!" Miss Prendergast sighed. "Of course we should have had an understudy. But nobody realized that there would be this—inconvenience. I imagine poor Hester is as heartbroken as anybody, in spite of the new baby."

"Is it a long part?"

"No, that's the worst of it!" She laughed. "I hope you follow me. What I mean is, it seems such a pity to have to give up the whole play just because one of the smaller parts can't be filled. It will be a lesson to us, I suppose. But meanwhile the children are frightfully disappointed."

An idea was forming in Anne's mind. She acted on it impulsively. "How would I do for the part?"

The teachers and the little girls stared at her.

"Do you *know* it? I thought I hadn't even mentioned the title," Miss Prendergast cried.

"Never laid eyes on it before—whatever it is," Anne said cheerfully. "But I love to act—at least I call it that— and any actress in a crisis. Besides, I'm a quick study. I've done a lot of it at college, and I learn fast. If you'll give me half an hour or so—"

"Oh, you'd save the day!" Miss Baker rejoiced. "No matter how bad you are you'll be wonderful!"

Anne laughed. "That's encouraging, and thanks! Suppose I get right at it, then."

They brought her a typewritten script. She glanced over it rapidly and saw that "Aunt Maria's" part wasn't very long: thirty speeches or so, none of them difficult.

"We can fix you up with clothes, fortunately," Miss Prendergast beamed. "Hester's things are here and, even if they don't quite fit, they'll do; we'll let out seams and pin you up again."

Anne slipped out of her dress and donned the plain gingham coveralls that were to have been Hester's. She screwed back her hair, and tied on the sunbonnet, and set a pair of glasses well down on her nose.

Little Janice screamed with excitement. "You're going to be lots better than Hester was"—she changed loyalty with the swiftness of children—" 'cause she never looked *old* enough for an aunt."

"I may look lots older before the play's over," Anne said merrily. "I may be positively doddering and wrinkled."

"How could you be?" Janice, evidently literal-minded, wanted to know. "The play only lasts a little while."

"It's not time," Anne said. "It's what time does to you." Janice looked more puzzled than ever, and Anne swooped down and patted her face. "Never mind, Janice; we'll see what happens."

She had an oddly excited feeling, and it communicated itself to the children and the teachers. They had been prepared—though unwillingly—to give up all thought of the play. And now, miraculously, here was deliverance from their dilemma. No matter how bad she was, she thought comfortably, she'd still be good enough. Because they would look at her that way. For now the play wouldn't have to be given up.

She went off in a corner and, bending over the script, tried to shut out the subdued murmurs of the children, consciously attempting to be very quiet so that she could get her part. The play was scheduled for eleven; if she could learn just the key speeches, and her cues, she could ad lib the rest, once she knew the sense of what she was to say. The cues were the most important part, for of course she couldn't expect the children to pick up an ad-libbed portion.

In the midst of her concentration a thought obtruded. Just a couple of days ago she had labeled "unorthodox" something that Miss Newton had done. Could anything be more unorthodox than this? Perhaps circumstances altered cases. And was this any part of an assistant librarian's duties? She had the absurd recollection of the phrase "outside the sphere of duty." Could she possibly put this down to such a wonderful definition as that? She wondered what the other librarians would say when they heard about it. And Miss Nichols. Would Miss Nichols approve? Or would she be up for a reprimand?

It was really too late to worry about it now. The die was cast. For the next hour she'd better concentrate on getting into the "feel" of Aunt Maria. After that she could worry about what she had done.

It was fun. It was more fun than she had ever imagined it could be. The children threw themselves with renewed vigor into their parts, so relieved were they that the play was to take place after all. They raced happily through their speeches; their actions were spontaneous and lively. The audience, sitting hunched up and eager-eyed, on the long benches in one of the cleared rooms, tittered and sighed gustily at all the right places. Only once did Anne falter; she had let her attention be distracted by one of her "nieces," pulling up a falling garter.

" 'I—I don't know why—' " she began, and stuck. To

cover it up, while she thought wildly, she invented some business: dusting off the table with vigorous motions—so vigorous, in fact, that she swept a china vase to the floor and broke it. "Oh, now look what I've done!" she cried. She meant it, but she realized that it made a good line. "That was the vase Uncle Henry brought from the fair . . . and now I've broken it!"

Little David stared at her. "Your uncle *didn't* bring it," he said stoutly. "That's my Mamma's, and she's going to be real mad that it's broke!"

Anne suppressed a giggle. This was clearly a moment of crisis. "Now, whatever got into me?" she cried. "I must be woolgathering. Of course that's your mother's vase, the one she lent me. And you just tell her I'll get her another."

David, somewhat pacified, slipped back into character.

The play swept on to its highly improbable but amusing close. Anne felt beads of perspiration on her upper lip and her face was flushed. She snatched off the close sunbonnet and the glasses, and ran her hands through her hair.

"Whew!"

The children crowded around her. "We like you!" Janice pronounced. "You were good. Miss Prendergast, can we ask her on the picnic too?"

The teachers were wringing her hands. "You were really a godsend! How shall we ever thank you? . . . Of course she's coming on the picnic. You *can* arrange it, can't you?" they appealed to her. "It's the very least we can do for you, and the children will be heartbroken if you don't come now. You're their new heroine."

Anne considered swiftly. After all, why not? The Cornell School had been the only place on her schedule and, if she took care of that, she had discharged her duties. Of course there would be library work afterward; but if she were late getting back she could stay late, and make it up on her own.

She said, "I'd love to come. And I'm so hungry I could eat a wolf."

With the children chattering like magpies as they flew in and out of the schoolhouse carrying books, they made short shrift of the library work. When the last book was in place, they locked the schoolhouse doors and set out, all of them, for the picnic spot. It was cool in the woodsy place they had chosen, and there was a brook gurgling near by. Anne was plied with sandwiches and homemade bread and cake and cookies and fruit until she was unable to move.

"Tell us a story!" some of the younger ones demanded, and she managed to shake off her torpor long enough to give them a condensed version of *The Cat Who Went to Heaven.*

Then she rolled over on her face and closed her eyes, letting the peace of the woods sink into her, with the children's voices growing more and more distant.

She woke with a feeling of utter content which not even the lateness of the hour could dispel. For the first time in weeks she felt rested and at peace. She sat up and shook herself.

"We played you were the Sleeping Princess while you were taking a nap," Janice announced with satisfaction. "We were all around you, but you never budged."

"Who was the Prince?" Anne wanted to know.

"David was," Janice said.

David looked sheepish. "Aw, they made me. . . . You were sorta big for me. You're awful long-stretched-out."

With their vociferous good-by's and thank-you's ringing in her ears, Anne sped back to Tilden. She had had no idea there would be experiences like that waiting for her on the road. Maybe the months wouldn't be all stodginess after all. But, she reminded herself cautiously, one swallow doesn't make a summer. She wondered suddenly if the Mouse had had anything comparable at Claremont. She was thinking smugly "How could she?" when she caught herself up sharply. What in the world was happening to her?

CHAPTER FIVE

〜〜〜

NINA LONSDALE ASKED WITH A WORRIED AIR, "DID you bring *Being Met Together*?"

"No," Anne said. "It was out. I'm sorry."

The little Harlowe librarian looked stricken. "Oh!" she moaned. "Oh, that's dreadful!"

Anne was bustling back and forth between shelves, but she stopped short. "Never mind, I'll surely have it next time."

"Next time won't do," Nina said tragically. "She wants to *now*."

"Who does?"

"Mrs. Twining."

"Well, Mrs. Twining will have to read something else meanwhile. There are lots of good new ones among those I brought. Give her one of those."

Nina Lonsdale said softly, "You don't know Mrs. Twining, do you?"

"No."

"You wouldn't say a thing like that if you did."

"Good heavens, what is she—a lady ogre?"

"She's . . . well . . ." Nina spread her hands. "She's everything. She's the richest woman in the neighborhood. She runs Harlowe—the Council, the Volunteer Fire Department, the Garden Club, the Library—"

"What!" Anne cried merrily. "Not the Red Cross?"

Nina Lonsdale was serious. "Oh, yes, I forgot. And the local Red Cross."

"How does she have time for all that?" Anne inquired, shoving books aside on the shelves to find space for the new ones.

"Oh, she has time all right!" Nina said bitterly. "Too much of it. She's as wealthy as a lady Croesus; has a simply beautiful place back in the hills—acres and acres, and a very old house full of antiques and heirloom lace and old fans and things like that."

"I know the type," Anne nodded. "I'll bet I know just what she looks like. Tall, regal manner, very grande dame, rustling silks and drop earrings and snow-white hair piled high . . ."

In spite of her anxiety Nina Lonsdale laughed. "You're wrong, all wrong! She *ought* to look like that, of course, but she doesn't. She's very short and has a shelfy bosom, iron-gray hair, and glasses; always wears tweeds and ghillies and old felt hats that look as if she had picked them up at a rummage sale. . . . Oh, good grief, she's coming!"

Nina's voice had sunk to a horrified whisper. Anne wheeled around. The screen door opened, slammed shut, and Mrs. Twining sailed down the corridor. She seemed to push the air away from her as she advanced, and Anne could imagine that any tangible object in her path would be just as effectively pushed aside.

"I'm in a hurry, Nina," she called as she came forward. "Are my books ready?"

Nina made a little sound that might have been assent. Anne knew that she was wondering how she could best break the news that one of the books hadn't come through.

"Well, speak out, girl!" Mrs. Twining ordered. Her

voice was the kind that would easily have filled a hall. "I told you to take down that silly sign 'Quiet, please'! It has a bad effect on you. There's no reason why you can't talk out in a library as well as in a butchershop. If people are so easily disturbed—" Her gaze fell on Anne. "Who's that?" she demanded.

"Oh—oh, yes." Nina was flustered. "Mrs. Twining, this is Miss McLane—Anne McLane. She's from Kenyon County Library."

"Never saw her before," Mrs. Twining said. There was a wealth of disapproval in her voice. "Where's Jessica Nichols?"

"Miss Nichols had a bad fall and broke her leg," Anne said.

Mrs. Twining slapped her hand down on the desk emphatically. "I knew it would happen! I told her time and time again that if she persisted in carrying so many books that she couldn't see over the top of them—"

"She fell downstairs," Anne inserted deftly. "At her home."

Mrs. Twining was stopped, but only momentarily. Her brows drew together. "Practically the same thing. Probably had on high heels and was hurrying with a load of something or other. Where is she now?"

"In the hospital," Anne said.

"Best place for her. They'll keep her quiet. I must say it's very hard on all of us. Are *you* taking her place?"

"Only partly. I'm an assistant, and I've had to take over the route because I drive."

"Silly of Jessica not to have other people there who could drive. I always told her so." It was obvious that one of

62

the crosses Mrs. Twining had to bear—and not silently—
was that people didn't always take her advice. She turned
to the librarian. "By the way, Nina, I shall want you to
come to luncheon next Monday. At one. There are a number
of things I want to talk to you about."

Nina flushed. "Thank you so much, Mrs. Twining; but,
really, I can't leave—"

"Nonsense. Of course you can."

"The Library opens at one, you know. From one to five-
thirty."

"Cross out the 'one' on the sign and put in 'two.' Just for
that day."

"But people—"

"Practically no one comes here from one to two, and
you know it. This is *very* important. Biddle will call for
you—and bring you back, of course."

"Oh dear, I don't see—"

"Are my books ready now? I really must fly."

"They're all here, Mrs. Twining, all except—"

Mrs. Twining's eyes popped ever so slightly. "Don't tell
me you didn't get the one I *particularly* asked for!"

"I did put in the request, Mrs. Twining. But Miss
McLane said it was out."

Mrs. Twining threw down the packet of books she had
picked up. "Really, this is too much! I shall have to do
something about it. Why in the name of goodness I can't
have an *occasional* book that I ask for, *when* I ask for it,
is beyond me. What happened to it? Where is it? Who
has it?"

Anne stepped into the breach. "Our station copy was at
Meadville," she said. "And our library copy was out on

loan. I'll try to bring it next time. That will only be a few weeks from now."

Mrs. Twining wheeled on her. "Young woman, I want to read it *now*."

Anne took a deep breath. "Then why don't you buy a copy?" she asked mildly.

"Well!" Mrs. Twining exploded. "Well! I have never heard anything *quite* like this!"

Nina was actually quailing behind the desk, as if she expected a physical blow to land on Anne's shoulders. Anne couldn't help smiling a bit, inwardly. Mrs. Twining did not terrify her.

"If it's so important to you to read it," she suggested, "I should think buying a copy would be the solution."

"I never buy a copy of a book until I have read it and am sure I want it in my library," Mrs. Twining explained. And then she said haughtily, "Though why I should enter into discussion with you—"

"I'm glad you did," Anne took her up. "It's a new idea to me. You see, I was thinking that, if you bought it and read it and didn't want it, you could give it to the Library, and that way add to their stock."

Mrs. Twining caught up her package of books once more. "I'm not in the habit of being dictated to," she announced. "And don't bother about the book. I'm not sure that I *want* to read it . . . after this."

"It's a good book," Anne said. "And it will still be a good book when I bring it next time."

Mrs. Twining ignored Anne, swept Nina with a disapproving glance, and sailed out.

At the door she called, without turning, "Monday, Nina, at one. I shall expect you."

64

There was a little silence after she left, the kind of silence that follows an eruption.

Nina said at last, weakly, "Phew! I don't see how you dared."

"It wasn't *your* fault," Anne said warmly. "I couldn't stand by and see you blamed. I only hope I didn't make things more difficult for you."

Nina gave a wan smile. "Oh, no," she quavered. "I'm—I'm rather used to her. But, oh, how I dread Monday!"

"Does she often order you up?"

"At intervals. Generally there's something she disapproves of or wants changed. Or she wants impossible things done. Heavens, I'd love to do lots of the things she suggests. But how can I on such a limited budget? It simply won't stretch any more—it's at the breaking point now."

"Why doesn't *she* do some of the things she wants done?"

"Mrs. Howard Winthrop Twining?" Nina asked, with lifted eyebrows. "She gets others to do things, and if they don't she gets disagreeable. But she doesn't do them herself . . . that's beneath her."

"Or maybe it never occurs to her," Anne suggested. "D'you know—all the time she was talking I kept thinking of my old school headmistress. Her name was Partridge, and we girls used to quail before her."

Nina laughed. "That's a fowl joke."

"Good for you! That's a ducky rejoinder! . . . This has gone far enough. I have to move on to Freedom Corners. Don't let La Twining get you down and I'll surely, surely, bring *Being Met Together* next time, if I have to steal it from whatever branch it's in."

"She said she doesn't want it any more, but I bet she will," Nina observed. She reached down under the desk and put back the small printed sign "Quiet, please" with a little click. "Now I feel better."

"Everybody has his problems," Anne thought as she drove along. "Even as I have."

She wondered why other people's problems always seemed simpler, easier of solution, than your own. If she were in Nina's place, she knew just what she'd do about Mrs. Twining. But if Nina were in her place, what could she do . . . except stick it out, exactly as she was doing?

You came upon Freedom Corners so swiftly that you were likely to miss it entirely. For miles there had been nothing but spreading farms. Then, all at once, there was a little church, a volunteer fire department, a gas station, and a small general store, and that was the village of Freedom Corners. Beyond the store the farmlands began again.

The library station was in the general store. Anne parked in the shade of an elm and went in. A bell tinkled when the screen door fell to behind her. Mounds of canned goods, a display tin of biscuits covered with cellophane, crates of fruit, half-opened barrels, and cans of kerosene. A fan twirled lazily in the ceiling. There was no one about, and Anne could see no sign of books anywhere.

"Is anyone here?" she asked, raising her voice and feeling silly.

There was no answer. Maybe the proprietor and his wife were taking a little time off for a midday siesta. There certainly didn't seem to be a rush of business. She ambled around the store, reading labels and poking her head behind the long wooden counters. At the rear of the store she half fell over an overturned carton, and twisted her ankle.

"Ouch!" she said aloud.

"Huh?" a voice came, startlingly near, and she found herself face to face with a tall gangling red-haired boy hunched on a stool with a book open on his lap. It was evident that he had been so lost in what he was reading that he hadn't heard her enter or call. "You want something?" he asked her now. "I'll be right there."

He stumbled up, laying the book carefully face down on the stool. His eyes had a faraway look; he was still lost in the printed page.

Behind him, Anne saw, were four shelves of books. "Is this the Library?" she said.

"Yep. Want a book? You new here? I know some good ones; I read 'em all," he volunteered eagerly.

"I've brought some new ones," she told him. "I'm from Kenyon County Library."

"*You* are?" He stared at her with frank curiosity. "Why, where's Miss Nichols?"

Anne explained about Miss Nichols.

"Gee," he said with real concern, "that's fierce. And she was gonna bring me a coupla special books."

The disappointment on his face was tragic.

"Maybe I have them on the truck," Anne said cheerfully. "I brought everything that was ordered. Want to come and see?"

"Gee!" he breathed again. "I been waiting for this day for weeks. I read all through the books, and then there's nothing . . . so I read 'em again." He pushed open a rear door. "Mrs. Polly!" he yelled. "The Library's here!"

"I thought the name was—Polachek," Anne said, consulting a card in her bag.

"Well, it is. But everybody calls 'em Mr. and Mrs. Polly

—for short, I guess. Mr. Polly's down to the Ration Board and Mrs. Polly's lookin' after her kid. She's lame; one leg's shorter'n the other. I mind her sometimes when Mrs. Polly's busy. Poor kid! She can't do anything like other kids, and she can't read either." He gave a gusty sigh. "I don't know what I'd do if I couldn't read. It sure takes you out of yourself!"

Mrs. Polachek bustled in. "Excuse me, please! I do not hear you. Berta she is restless today. She wants to be out. But how can I be out and also in?"

"Well, gee, Mrs. Polly, I said I'd look after the customers. Only there weren't any. You coulda stayed as long as you wanted."

Mrs. Polachek's round face crinkled in distaste, and her eyes were somber. "But I do not want! Berta she cries all the time, 'Mama, why don't we do this? Mama, let's do that! Mama, I'm tired of my dolls.' I go crazy!"

"Poor child!" Anne was sympathetic. "It must be hard for her. Does she like to use her hands?"

"She does not like to crochet." Mrs. Polachek was disapproving. "I try to teach her. Me, I was the best one for crochet in my whole village. I won the prize, and I crochet everything—lace, and bedspreads and tablecloths and all. But Berta she will not learn."

"Sewing, perhaps?" Anne suggested.

"For her dolls she sews, or what she calls sews." Mrs. Polachek shrugged. "But all her dolls they have more clothes now than they can use; so she does not care for that any more." She gave a lugubrious sigh. "My boy he is big and strong. Berta is so little and weak. And maybe she does not walk any more. The doctor he says nothing. How it will be when she grows old I do not know."

"You mustn't give up hope," Anne said. "They do such wonderful things nowadays. Have you taken her to New York, or Newark?"

"For such trips I do not have money," Mrs. Polachek said firmly. "And time. And it makes Berta tired. . . . Well," she said then, "if you want to change the books, you go ahead. Charlie here will help you. I do not know why I keep this station. It takes up space where I could put canned goods, and not many people come for books. Mostly it is Charlie."

"Oh gee, Mrs. Polly, you wouldn't give up the station!" he begged. "You're always sayin' that. But you don't really mean it, do you?"

"How do I know?" She sounded a little cross. "Money it doesn't bring in, and it takes room in the store. And the people who come for books—I can't see that they buy more than those who do not."

"I'll help you change 'em," Charlie offered to Anne. "I always help Miss Nichols. She says I'm good. I can carry a lot at a time, and then she lets me choose the ones that are to be kept here."

Anne smiled. "All right, Charlie; let's get going. I'm Anne McLane, just for reference."

He watched her open up the truck and pull out the shelves as if she were a conjurer evoking wonderful delights for his particular pleasure.

"Look at 'em! A lot here I never saw before! Gee, that's swell!"

"Is everybody in your family as keen about reading as you are?" Anne asked, busily sorting cards.

"Naw!" He laughed. "Pa thinks I'm crazy. And Ma doesn't say much; but I guess she sorta does, too. And my sister—well, she's got a boy friend and that's all *she* thinks about. Wouldn't waste her time reading, she says. . . . Well, everybody to his own taste. I read that, somewhere. They sure don't know what they're missin'."

He lowered his voice confidentially. "You know what? Mrs. Polly could have a lot more people takin' books if she wanted to. She doesn't go at it right. She has the shelves hidden, and the space is so narrow, anyhow, that fat ladies can't get in. One tried it once and got stuck, and I guess the news spread. She ought to put the case out in the middle of the store and put a sign up—you know, like they do for food. 'Have you read So and So?' . . . 'Special for today—Such and Such.' Display a different book every day. Call attention to 'em! Gosh, everything's advertising these days; you'd think she would get hep!"

"You have something there, Charlie," Anne assured him solemnly. "Have you ever suggested it to her?"

"Say, have you ever tried suggestin' anything to Mrs. Polly? . . . Well, of course not; you're new here. But there's no use—take it from me. She's got her own ideas. And not too many of 'em. Besides, I don't want to rile her; she lets me choose the books off the Bookmobile and that's somethin'!"

He was peering eagerly along the shelves, pulling out book after book with an unerring hand. "Yep . . . and here are the two I wanted. *Digging in Yucatan* and *Land below the Wind*. I can hardly wait to sink my teeth in 'em."

"Are you going to be a writer, Charlie?"

"Me? I should say not!" he laughed with infectious mirth. "That's hard work. I'm going to be an engineer, a civil engineer. I want to go places!"

"But—" Anne began.

"You never heard of a civil engineer gettin' stuck in one spot longer'n awhile, did you? Well, that's me. I'll be earnin' a livin', and every once in a while I'll take a spell off and go see the places I didn't get sent to! I've got it all planned. First off, I'm goin' around the world. That's so's I can decide which places I want to go back to. I'll work my way over and around in the summers between college. I guess the war'll be over by that time . . . worse luck. Lots of the kids at school want to be pilots or bombardiers, but there won't be room for all of 'em later. Me, I'm going into a job that's got a future! They'll always need civil engineers."

"You *have* got it all planned," Anne said admiringly.

"Sure," he said with complacence. "Why not? You gotta know where you're headin' these days; you might as well start early. . . . Yep, and here's one we want too."

He withdrew a book from the shelf.

Anne peered over his shoulder. *"Map-Making in the United States,"* she said doubtfully. "Do you think many people will want that?"

"Nope," he answered promptly. "Hardly anybody, I guess, but me. *I* want to read it."

Anne laughed. "I think I won't call this Freedom Corners any more. I'm going to call it Charlie's Station."

A grin spread over his freckled face. "I'll bet that's what folks think anyhow. . . . Say, at that, you better pick out some books you think we oughta have. Otherwise Mrs. Polly's apt to do what she says—give up the station entirely."

He helped Anne carry in the books, keeping up a running fire of comment on them and on his future plans. "Listen," he said, wiping the sweat off his forehead, "this is hot work. C'mon and have a coke. On me!" he added grandly.

"Charlie, I'd love one. But not on you."

"Sure on me. I've got some money. Mrs. Polly pays me for sittin' around here. Might as well spend it in her store."

He went behind a counter, dug into the red container, and came up with two bottles. "Ice-cold!" He removed the caps neatly, handed her a straw. "See you in Cairo!" he toasted, and tipped up the bottle.

"Here's to Istanbul!" Anne returned.

"And Port Said," he added.

"Not to mention Madagascar."

"Betcha I'll get to all those places yet."

"Charlie," she assured him gravely, "it's not fair to bet on a sure thing."

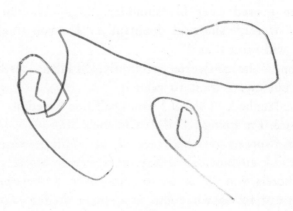

CHAPTER SIX

ANNE THUMPED THE CUSHIONS INTO A FLUFFY HEAP and threw herself back on them with a contented sigh. The porch glider resumed its comfortable creaking, and she gazed up through the interlacing maple branches at the stars glittering in the summer sky.

"Anybody home?" came a voice from the darkness.

"Advance, brother, and give the countersign," Anne said.

"Ginger ale."

"Come up, Rex, and find yourself a chair. Don't stumble over the footstool. Oh, and my knitting bag's down there somewhere."

"Booby traps?"

"Are you a booby?" she inquired gaily. "What are you doing in these parts?"

"What do you think—inspecting the forts?"

"If you stopped in for ginger ale, you'll have to find it yourself. I'm too comfortable to move."

"The perfect hostess," he murmured. "A drink was only incidental. I thought I might find some stimulating conversation . . . and possibly a dancing partner."

"Oh, it's too hot to dance, Rex. Wouldn't you rather just sit and be the brilliant conversationalist yourself? I'm a willing listener."

"Where's everybody?"

"They've gone to the movies. They couldn't *bribe* me to go along. In fact, I think parents should have a night off occasionally. Don't you?"

"Depends on the offspring."

"Hmmmm. We won't go into that."

"I was going to be very complimentary," he countered. "But now it sounds to me as if you had a guilty conscience. What've you been doing with yourself since I saw you last?"

"Working. Early and late. That's why I appreciate these cushions so much."

"Too bad you have to slave like that. You're very decorative there on those cushions."

"How can you tell? It's as black as ink."

"I can have observed before, can't I?" he said reasonably. "And quite pleasant to remember, too, if I may say so. . . . But somehow I can't just picture you in a Bookmobile."

She laughed. "It's not as relaxed as this—I can tell you that much. One eye on the gas gauge, one eye on the road, my mind running ahead to the next station . . . and, when I get there, unloading books by the hundreds, and meeting people, and loading them in again—the books, I mean—"

He clucked sympathetically. "Sounds as if you needed a porter."

"Oh, I do have help. The boys are awfully nice. And then once in a while you run into somebody special . . . like this afternoon." She began telling him about Charlie. Recalling his vivid hair and enthusiasm, she drew him in swift, telling sentences. "He's going to escape from Freedom Corners. He's already escaping. It made me realize how much books can mean to people like that. Charlie's going places. He has his life all mapped out." She gave herself a hunch on

74

the cushions and sat up. "What are *you* going to do after the war, Rex?"

He stretched and put his arms back of his head. "Lord knows. I may have had ideas once, but they're shelved for the duration. And maybe beyond."

"Why?"

"Why not? What's the use of planning?" he demanded. "People plan like mad . . . and what happens? Along comes a war, or something equally catastrophic, and where are their plans? Knocked into a cocked hat. Nope, it's better to drift along with the stream. If it throws you up on some pleasant shore, O. K. If not—" There was a shrug in his voice. "At least you aren't disappointed."

"But the work you're in—" Anne prodded.

"Stopgap. I was shoved into it. I do it the best I can—and I'm not saying I'm not bored stiff with it, too, most of the time—and that's that. Afterward—well, if anybody offers me a pleasant little island with a coffeebush and a pecan tree, I'll take it. I've a lot of loafing to get out of my system."

"But there'll be so much to do after the war, Rex!" Anne cried, with sudden vigor. She sat erect now, pushing the hair out of her eyes. "You see it more and more every day. A whole world to rebuild. It's tremendous! Everybody—everybody's talents—will be needed!"

"Count me out," he said lazily. "There'll be plenty of earnest workers to do the job, and to get into each other's hair. Everybody with a pet project of his own, and ideas as to how it should be carried through! Gosh, what a madhouse it's going to be! That little island is going to be a refuge all right!"

"You're joking."

"Never more serious in my life."

Anne was silent a moment; then she said carefully, "What were you doing before the war?"

"I was in a brokerage house. The fair-haired boy. I thought maybe I'd make a fortune in the stock market in my off moments, but it didn't work out that way. And then I thought maybe the president would take a fancy to me and groom me for his job, but his daughter got married and so, of course, son-in-law was slated for the cushioned seat." He laughed. "Maybe it was just as well. It was a boring kind of life. Buying and selling. Accounting. Shorts and longs. And I always did hate fractions!"

"All right, if you don't want to talk about it." Anne sat up. "You're probably training for a secret mission, and no details are to be given out. I'll get your drink."

"No, honestly, Anne," he protested. "Why should I have to be serious? Everybody else is. That's not my nature. I wouldn't be any good stewing about the future of the world, and I know it. I'm fundamentally lighthearted, and if the war's over soon enough I'll still be that way . . . I hope."

"I hope so, too," she said gently, after a moment.

It was queer—he was years older than she, but just now she felt that she was the older of the two. And yet light-hearted people *were* needed . . . and he was fun.

Perhaps, she decided, it was because she had so many things on her mind. That was queer, too . . . how many things stayed with her about her work.

"I find myself thinking about the Library, and the people I've met, and the books they ought to read, long after six

76

o'clock," she told Miss Nichols on her next visit to the hospital.

Miss Nichols lay in a high white bed, with her leg in a canvas cradle to which were attached ropes that ran through pulleys on the ceiling. There were beads of perspiration on her lip; but she smiled sweetly, and sniffed with appreciation at the flowers Anne had brought her.

"It's not fair, is it?" she asked. "Particularly since there is no time and a half for overtime in library work."

Anne gave her a startled grin. "You took the words right out of my mouth! Are all jobs like that—making you think about them after quitting?"

"I don't know. I suppose it depends on how interested you are. Tell me, how are you getting on?"

Anne spread her hands a little. Her mouth was rueful. "I wish I could give you a glowing report. But all I've gathered so far is that I'm not Miss Nichols! I can't blame them for resenting me a little."

"They don't resent *you*, my dear," Jessica Nichols said patiently. "They resent my falling downstairs." She gave a sudden little laugh. "I resent it myself, more and more! To think of having to spend a whole summer here!"

"They miss you very much," Anne said. "I hear it at every turn, and I have a lot of messages for you."

"Yes, people have been sweet," the librarian answered. "It makes me feel good to get all these cards"—she waved her hand to the bedside table—"and these delicacies. Look, aren't they tempting? I'm glad nothing's the matter with my stomach." She pointed out the gifts: a jar of crab-apple jelly from Mrs. Thomas, a box of cookies from Miss Lemuel, jellied broth from Mrs. Horvath; and there were games and a bed jacket and puzzles. . . . "I'll have a very good time if I can pull myself away from counting the slats in the Venetian blinds!" Miss Nichols said. "But do you know something—not one person has sent me a book!"

Anne laughed. "I suppose they think it would be carrying coals to Newcastle!"

They talked of all kinds of things, but Jessica Nichols seemed to make a point of not asking Anne about her contacts outside the County Library itself. Anne couldn't decide whether she wasn't interested, or whether she felt comparisons might be odious, or whether she wanted her assistant to make all her own discoveries. And then it was time to go.

So Anne was decidedly unprepared for Miss Ada Howland at Janeway. She was buxom and vivacious, with high-piled blond hair that was trying to turn gray but was not permitted to do so by Miss Howland. She had flashing teeth, several of which were banded with gold, and she wore dangling earrings and an amazing assortment of colors in her clothes. The Library at Janeway was a converted blacksmith shop. Extra windows had been cut in the walls, and the forge was now a mammoth fireplace. Bookshelves stood against the blackened walls, and the uneven floor was laid, in spots, with rag rugs. Miss Howland enveloped her in an encompassing smile and a torrent of words.

Anne learned, in short order, that she "adored" her work; that she had been dying of ennui out here in the country when this job was offered her, and it had literally saved her reason.

"I used to be an actress, you know," she confided, with an arch movement of her head. "Don't ask me when . . .

it was a thousand years ago; but I *must* show you my clippings, my dear, if you're interested. George Cohan and William Gillette and Ada Rehan were all my friends. . . . There, I've given myself away! If you're any good at all you'll figure out how old I am at once! But, of course, I started as a mere slip of a girl. My mother was an actress before me—I was born when she was on the road and she carried me in a trunk tray, *exactly* like in books, my dear— and I simply *imbibed* the atmosphere of the theater along with my milk."

She patted the blond hair expertly. "Oh, I did have a good time! Not that it isn't a hard life—it's terribly hard, and I wouldn't recommend it to a soul unless she had a constitution of iron. . . . But it didn't do me any harm. In fact, I say I'm healthier than a lot of these women around here who've gone to bed at nine every night and had their vitamins and fresh air and exercise according to the best doctors. It's all in your *attitude,* I say. Now I loved my art, so I thrived on it. That's essential, don't you think?"

She paused for the briefest fraction of a second, and Anne gulped, "Yes. Oh, yes, indeed."

Whereupon Miss Howland flowed on, with a bright nod of appreciation. "Exactly. I worked for years and then I met George. Of course I had slews of suitors, and it was awfully hard to choose; but George had *everything* . . . I thought. So I chose him and married him and came out here to live. I didn't regret it for a minute."

She looked at Anne brightly; and Anne stared back, fascinated.

"You might think I would have missed the lights and the crowds and the applause, but I didn't . . . for I had George.

He was so sweet. He had a big estate out here, and he wanted to be a gentleman farmer." She threw back her head and laughed. "Poor darling . . . he could have been anything else, I suppose. But he simply was not cut out for a farmer. His superintendent gypped him, and he sank his money in blooded cattle and newfangled silos and all kinds of machinery that was never used . . . and then came the stock-market crash, and the bank holiday. And, well"——she threw out her hands in a theatrical but very effective gesture—— "that simply *finished* us, my dear!"

Ada Howland had a splendid sense of timing; she waited just long enough so that Anne was compelled to ask "And then what happened?" before she swept on.

"*Well* . . . I wasn't a bit downhearted, but George was. He was sunk. The place went to pot, and he was so gloomy, poor sweet lamb, that I think it had a lot to do with his getting pneumonia. We couldn't pull him out of it, and he died. I was heartbroken, but I have a very ebullient nature and I did rally. One *has* to go on living. So I sold the place and bought a darling little house in the village and twiddled my thumbs, wondering if I should go back to the stage—though I hated to work so hard again at my age—when they started the Library and I just *jumped* at the chance of being in charge.

"Of course I didn't know a thing about books; but I was a great reader and was terribly fond of them, and no one else seemed to have the time, and the salary was *so* tiny . . . so I got it, after all. And," she concluded triumphantly, "I've had it ever since! People are used to me by this time, and I just love my work. I'm full of it. Here, take off your hat and let me show you my domain. I'm dying to fix up this ell."

She piloted Anne to a door in the far wall and threw it open. A bare whitewashed room with sanded floor met her eyes.

"It doesn't look like much, but you should have *seen* it before. Dirty and cluttered and horrible! I worked like a slave to clear it up, and Mr. Jaspers painted it for me, and Mr. Kinney did the floor. I'm going to have a children's room there if it's the last thing I do! And it *won't* be—the last thing, I mean."

Anne asked, "Are there lots of children?"

Miss Howland waved her hands expressively. "Millions. They swarm in from the whole village. Everything's too high for them—the tables and chairs, even most of the shelves. They sit on the floor often, and I tell them stories. I love to have children around me. You see"—her voice deepened and softened—"I never had any of my own."

She closed the door again and stood with her back to it. "I know you've been wondering why I'm Miss Howland. It was my stage name, and I'm used to it. I loved being Mrs. George Langley, but after George died I went back to my first name—it seemed more right, somehow. Because I *wasn't* Mrs. George Langley, with him gone."

Janeway was a busy station. The screen door banged continually with customers coming and going. Ada Howland, in spite of her tendency to talk, proved to be an efficient librarian, and her good nature was boundless. She had a smile and a word—or a torrent of words—for everyone. She seemed to know everything that was going on in the neighborhood—all the latest gossip, just how many there were in each family, who had been sick, who had been away—and her friendly inquiries and her bright interest made a pleasant atmosphere in the old shop.

Anne listened as she worked. Ada Howland never had a derogatory word to say about any book.

"Yes, *do* read it; I'm sure you'll enjoy it. And let me know how you like it." . . . "Oh, *that's* good . . . yes, take it by all means." . . . "You'll love this one; I'm so glad you chose it."

In a lull she turned to Anne. "I suppose you wonder why I'm so uncritical. You know, my idea is—let people read. Encourage them to read. I want them to feel free in here to pick out absolutely any book at all and take it home with them. If you get them to like to read, you can do something about their taste if you want to. But if they won't even get the habit—"

"You're wise," Anne said, smiling. "I've often thought that."

"I never did see, anyhow," Miss Howland said, with a shake of her blond head, "why a librarian should get hot and bothered because everybody isn't panting to read *Bureaucracy—a Challenge to Better Management,* or something like that, that she considers a good book. If a person wants to read light romances, he has a need for light romances. If he wants mysteries, then mysteries he shall have. People read for different reasons; it's not up to *me* to decide which way they should go . . . unless they want me to. And, besides," she said stoutly, "there are only good books in this library; so I don't have to worry *what* they read!"

Riding back toward Tilden, Anne thought about the rather unusual Ada Howland. She liked her. There was a woman who had taken what life offered and found it good. But, Anne decided, she was the kind of woman who would find interest and pleasure in whatever she was doing, in whatever circumstances she found herself. There was as much philosophy in that as in her philosophy about how to run a library.

It had been cool in the old blacksmith shop. Or perhaps, because she was so interested in Ada Howland, she hadn't noticed the heat. But now, facing the sun, feeling it beat in on her arms and legs, she was uncomfortably conscious of how hot it was. Heat waves shimmered up from the radiator cap, danced along the road, wavered over the scenery. It was peaceful, lovely scenery, but she was in no frame of mind to enjoy it. Oh, for a dish of ice cream . . . a long cool lemonade . . . a coke—even a glass of water! Yes, more than anything else, a glass of water! The more she thought about it and the seeming impossibility of getting it until she reached Tilden, the more she wanted it. Her throat scratched and burned; she had difficulty in swallowing.

How stupid! She'd stop at a farmhouse and *ask* for a glass of water. The very next one. The very next one, she promised herself, and found her thirst growing more bearable.

It was a long time in materializing, and then Anne's heart fell in dismay. She had said she'd stop here, but she didn't want to. It was a small house, tumble-down, ill-kempt; hardly more than a shack really. Its shutters sagged dispiritedly; one end of the roof sagged; the gate sagged on its rusty hinges. Uneven black letters on the rural mailbox spelled "Willem Harmsma." She sat for a moment debating what to do. Should she pretend she hadn't said "the very next one"? But that was being childish. No matter how disreputable the house looked, there must be water . . . and at the mere thought of the word, her tongue clove to the roof of her mouth.

She jumped down, then, and opened the gate. It squeaked in protest, as if it were unused to being pushed open. There was a rocking chair on the porch, and a palm-leaf fan beside it on the floor. Someone must be home, but there was no other sign of life. The blinds at the two front windows were drawn; there was absolute quiet all about. Determinedly, though, Anne raised her fist and pounded on the door. She waited a minute and tried again.

Perhaps whoever lived here was in the garden . . . though "garden" was hardly the word to describe the tangle of tall grass and flowers gone to seed and overrun fencing that surrounded the house. She walked around the little dirt footpath to the rear of the shack. There were old crates and a half-demolished barrel and a broken-down bench against the house wall. A grapevine sprawled over a rickety trellis, and two lean white chickens came forth from a small coop and eyed her indifferently before they began to peck with languor in the dust.

Anne's nose wrinkled in distaste and she turned to go.

"Get out of here, whoever you are!" a gruff voice called from the doorway.

Anne wheeled, startled and angry. A tall man with gray hair and dark glasses leaned against the doorframe. His face had a bitter, sardonic look; his mouth was grim.

She said coldly, "I'm just going. I'm sorry I bothered you."

"What do you want?" he demanded.

His voice had the rasp of an old saw. Why should he care what she wanted, if he was ordering her off the place?

"I wanted a glass of water," she retorted, "but I don't any more."

"You certainly knocked to raise the dead," he commented acidly.

Anne's temper flared. "Then why didn't you answer?"

"Because I don't want anybody around," he shot back. "That ought to be clear enough to anyone who can see. . . . *I* can't."

Anne put a hand to her face. "Oh," she said. "I'm sorry. I'm terribly sorry."

"I didn't ask for your pity!"

"I wasn't giving you pity," she said with spirit. "If you can't tell the difference between that and sympathy— And I'm sorry I disturbed you. I'll be on my way now."

His belligerent figure eased a little, surprisingly. "If you want a drink, come in and get it," he said. He moved aside in the doorway, and when she hesitated he cried out, "Come inside! Help yourself! Everything's in plain view."

He was a difficult, an impossible, man. But now she understood what lay back of it. That made a difference. She stepped across the sill. The inside of the little house was so dim it made her blink a bit. But she saw at once that everything was extremely neat. The contrast to the outside was startling. The boards were scrubbed, the rag rugs washed to a faded softness, shelves arranged precisely, chairs against the wall. There was a kind of bare simplicity that spoke as loudly as words. No extraneous details, no things to trip unwary feet; only what was *needed;* nothing just to look at and enjoy.

She found a tumbler and pushed the pump handle up and down. A gush of cold water filled the glass, and she drank thirstily.

"Oh, that was good!" she said impulsively. "I don't think I've ever tasted better water. I was simply parched."

She dried the glass carefully on the towel hanging above the sink, and put it back where she had found it.

The man said, "You came in some kind of truck. It sounded like a fairly light truck, but well loaded."

"It's a Bookmobile," she told him. "Loaded with books, of course. I'm from Kenyon County Library."

She happened to be looking at him, with her innocent words, and was horrified to see his face crumple up like a child's; it twitched with a passing pain, and he bit his lips.

"Books!" he exploded. "I lived on books. And I'll never be able to read a book again."

She put out her hand in an involuntary gesture. "Isn't there any—"

"Hope?" he took her up savagely. "Not a ray. The future's as black as this room . . . for me. It's queer. I never asked much of life. Enough work to keep me in money, enough money to buy books, enough leisure to read them. And here I sit. A lump! A dead man. I might as well be dead. I wish to God I were!"

The air vibrated with the ferocity of his words. Anne stood still in the middle of the kitchen. What was there to say?

But her sympathy must have flowed out to him, for all at once he said, so suddenly that she jumped, "Sit down!"

She collapsed onto the nearest chair, and he groped his way to a large rocker with padded seat.

"I suppose you're wondering why I'm stuck out here," he said after a moment. "I haven't talked to anyone for so long I might as well talk to you—now that I've begun." One corner of his mouth lifted briefly. "It's good to talk a little. I'd forgotten how good it is."

"I wish you *would* tell me," she said gently.

"I worked in Passaic. Dull sort of job, but it paid. I was saving enough to do a little research on the side; I had something in mind I wanted to try out. . . . Well," he said after a moment, "I tried it. This is the result"—his hand lifting to his eyes.

"I guess my world sort of fell to pieces. I was half mad with fury—with frustration. I'd inherited this shack a long time before; never did much about it except come out for week ends of loafing and fishing. After—this happened, I decided to come out for good; hide from the world." One lean hand stroked his hair with a nervous gesture. "I did a pretty thorough job of it, apparently. After a while nobody from my old world seemed to care whether I was alive or dead."

Anne said slowly, "Didn't people here—"

"Oh, sure," he answered bitterly. "At first. Out of curiosity. I couldn't blame them, but I hated them for it. After I—bit a few, so to speak, they left me alone. I do pretty well for myself. The place probably looks shot to pieces outside, but what of it? Inside's all I need care about." He pushed back the rocker so violently that it scraped against the wall, and Anne automatically noted the black mark it made on the whitewash. "All I wanted was a chance to read . . . and there's no chance of that, ever." His voice rose. "It's like being in prison. In eternal darkness. Nothing to do but wait for the end. Did you ever know how long a day can be? As long as a night. Endless."

Anne twisted her hands together. The man's bitterness cut into her. It was understandable, but it wasn't right, it was too deep, too hopeless. There must be something for him, some way of alleviating his darkness.

She tried hesitantly, "Did you ever ask someone to come in and read to you?"

He laughed, a harsh unpleasant laugh. "Lord, yes! I hired a woman, a man, a couple of kids. One was as bad as the other. Terrible voices, slovenly, no rhythm or beauty. They made a travesty of the words. I couldn't stand it; I fired 'em all. . . . Since then it's been—a blank."

"Yes," Anne thought, "I could see that. A poor reader, one who hesitated over words, or mispronounced them, who had no feeling for the sentences he was reading, would drive anyone with a sensitive ear to distraction."

"The radio might help," she suggested.

"Wouldn't have one in the house," he shot back. "Even if I had electricity, which I haven't. . . . Drivel, most of it; and I can't listen all day just to hear a few gems, whenever they come on. Soap operas, liver-pill commercials, adenoidal tenors, and beery politicians—"

Anne giggled. "I know how you feel. There seem to be more attractions to turn off than to turn on." Then she sobered. "A Seeing Eye Dog—"

"No money," he said briefly. "And for what? Where would I go? What would I do? I'm too old to learn Braille, learn a new trade." She made a sound of protest, but he did not hear her. "And I don't want to go around the countryside collecting subscriptions."

She stood up then. He made it difficult, but she could not tell him so. He lashed out at the world because of his inner hurt; he was a bruised spirit; it was better that he should talk this way than keep it forever bottled up.

"I wish I could think of something to help," she said. "I know there *is* something."

"A new pair of eyes," he said with concentrated bitterness. "Get me those, and I'll ask nothing further of the world."

She went to the door and opened it again. How good the world looked—the world of sunshine and shadow, of green and blue and brown and rose! The willow bending in the breeze; the chicken scratching in the dust. Even the crates and barrel and broken-down bench leaped at her eager eyes and were devoured by them.

He followed her out. "If—if you ever ride by this way again," he said awkwardly, "I wish you'd stop in a moment. Pass the time of day with me. I'd—I'd appreciate it."

She turned with swift compassion and put her hand on his arm. "I will," she said. "And thank you for the drink. It was very refreshing."

"You have refreshed me, too," he said.

His words went with her out to the car, echoed in her ears. "You have refreshed me, too." What a beautiful thing to say!

CHAPTER SEVEN

LITTLE MISS NEWTON PECKED OVER THE NEW BOOKS LIKE
a bird looking for a particularly delectable worm.

She gave an ecstatic squeak. "Oh, you *did* bring it!" she
chirped, holding up *Beneficent Soil Bacteria and Plant Enzymes*. "I was sure you would. Isn't that the most awful
title? And it's as heavy as it looks." Then her face fell as
quickly as it had brightened. "But, oh, dearie me, that poor
Matt English will be so disappointed!"

"Why?" Anne wanted to know.

She was a little abstracted, trying to regain her former
knowledge of Miss Carrie Newton's enigmatic code system
and also to fathom several new combinations of letters that,
so far at least, seemed to defy solution.

"He thought yesterday was the day you came; so he drove
in—all the way in, the poor dear—and then when he found
it was *today* . . . I did feel so sorry for him. You see, he
won't be able to get in for another week at least. His
mother's not very well, and he has so much to look after
on the farm."

Anne thought rapidly. "I—I suppose I could drop it there
when I go home," she said tentatively.

Carrie Newton regarded her with a benevolent smile. "I
knew you'd think of it! Of course I wouldn't have dreamed

of suggesting it, but since you yourself— Now I could mark it right down here on his card . . ."

She pulled a card out of the cardboard box on her desk with more agility than Anne had imagined possible, and scribbled down a group of letters. Anne was unable to restrain her curiosity. She peered over Miss Newton's shoulder. C. L. D. P. Anne knitted her brows and thought prodigiously. "County Librarian" for C. L. That was easy—almost too easy. Miss Newton wasn't quite up to the mark. But D. P. What was that? Suddenly it came to her. "Delivered Personally." Of course!

"Eureka!" she cried.

Miss Newton wheeled around. "What did you say, dear?"

"Eureka, I have found it!" Anne repeated wickedly.

"Oh, the book you were looking for. . . . One is always looking for a book in a library, isn't one? Now, I'll lay this aside; and don't forget it. I know he'll be so pleased. And it *is* sweet of you to take it. But, of course, it's not out of your way and, after all, that's what a county library is for, and it isn't as if you had to use your own gas . . ."

Eventually Anne got away. Miss Newton had reversed her earlier judgment—it became almost embarrassingly evident—and now accepted Anne as a worthy successor to Miss Nichols, even if only temporary. Perhaps her digestion was better, or familiarity had bred a kind of trust; or perhaps the weather had something to do with it. Whatever it was, she made Anne's visit a series of little confidences, gossip items, and ejaculations of pleasure or disgust that Anne found highly amusing and somewhat distracting. It took her longer than she had expected to get through her work; but at the end of the morning she was the repository for an assortment of information, character sketches, and petty incidents that amazed her as she went over them, sorting and reclassifying them on the road toward Elmway.

She turned in the long drive, admiring again the stately trees that led in an arch of green to the white house with its gay red shutters. Just as she was debating whether to risk disturbing Mrs. English by knocking, a figure came toward her from the barn. When he recognized the car he broke into a run.

"I brought you some light reading," Anne called. "Special delivery." She leaned down under the seat. "And some grapes for your mother. How is she?"

"She's better, thanks; but she's asleep, I think. I'll make sure. She wouldn't want to miss you. . . . That was awfully good of you. I . . . I'd been hoping—"

"I know. Miss Newton said you were so disappointed not to get the book when you were in Gansville."

"I didn't mean that," he said deliberately. "I meant I was hoping you'd find a reason to stop in one of these days."

Anne felt herself flushing. "Well," she said hastily, "this was an urgent case. It's not according to rules at Library School exactly—but, then, I gather lots of things in actual practice aren't. And, after all, if a person wants a book and you can get it to him—" She broke off, laughing. "Kenyon County Library's motto is 'We Aim to Please.' Or at least it will be from now on!"

He was riffling eagerly through the pages. "I was anxious to get hold of this. It looks good."

"I hope it isn't as heavy reading as it feels."

"It's just the title," he told her. "I want to bone up a bit.

You see, I'm supposed to give a talk at the next Grange meeting."

"On *that* title?"

He grinned. "No, on that subject. I'm just going to call it 'Getting More Out of Your Ground.' That shouldn't scare anybody off."

"Are you a Grange member?" Anne asked.

He nodded. "Youngest—and brashest, maybe. They've been awfully decent about letting me spout off my ideas, just the same. We're pretty active around here, you know. And one of the oldest granges in the state."

"What I don't know about the Grange would fill a shelf of books. I wish you'd give me a five-minute digest of your aims and policies before I drive on. I've been collecting information all morning—I'd like to end up with a bang."

"Look here," he said, "have you had lunch?"

"No. You think I'll need it before you can start your lecture?"

"I was thinking—Mother'll be asleep. Why can't you have lunch here? Everything's fixed. We could take our stuff out on the porch, or eat under the apple trees. Would you?"

Anne said, after a moment, "I'd love it. And I give you fair warning—I have a tremendous appetite." She got down and stretched. "Can I help?"

"Come along," he said. "What would you like to drink?"

"Isn't milk the only answer on a farm?"

"Not on this farm. The right answer is exactly what you really want."

"Well, then, iced tea, if it's possible."

"It's possible if you make the tea to suit yourself. I'll shake out the ice cubes. . . . First, though, I'll see about

Mother." He tiptoed into the bedroom, came back a moment later and closed the intervening door behind him. "She's still asleep. It's doing her a lot of good." He crossed to the refrigerator. "Now . . . here's a bowl of salad; vegetable by its appearance. How about it?"

"Bring it out."

"And some sliced tongue. Like it?"

"Love it."

"There's fresh bread, I know. And coconut cake."

"Cut me a huge wedge; it's my favorite kind."

"Hey, I've a thought! I'll put on a kettle of water, and go out and pull some corn. It'll be the first of the season."

"Oh, glory! Will there be plenty of butter to go with it?"

"All you can eat. It's Mrs. Lambkin's best, than which there is none better."

Anne giggled. "Mrs. Lambkin's Better Butter. I could do something with that. Or has she already done it?"

"It probably never occurred to her. I'll be back in a flash. Watch the kettle."

Anne busied herself with putting their meal on trays, hunting silver and napkins, setting aside the tea to brew. When Matt came back, he husked the corn expertly.

"Mm," she said admiringly, "it looks good enough to eat raw."

They plunged it into the boiling water, "Not longer than three minutes!" he warned. "This corn took special growing. I won't have it ruined."

"Will you sit on the ground, or will you be a sissy and have to have a chair?" he asked when, with trays piled high, they started out toward the orchard.

"What dare I say after that? But if I catch my death on

the ground, the family will sue you—since I won't be here to do it myself."

"I'm not worried," he returned. "The sun's been shining for a week. Do you good."

"Now," she said when they were settled. She sat tailor-fashion, the tray beside her. "Tell me about the Grange, and don't expect more than Umps and Hmps—I'll be too busy eating."

"What do you expect *me* to do—talk while I eat, or just not eat?"

She laughed. "Go on, one way or the other. I'm panting to learn."

"Well," he said, "first off it's not the Grange. That's only the name given the locals. The proper name is the Order of Patrons of Husbandry."

"That's impressive."

"It's a secret order, you know. Or did you?"

She turned to stare at him. "It *is*? Like the Masons? I had no idea. Why?"

He grinned. "Who am I to say? It began a long time ago—in Andrew Jackson's time. He sent a Mr. Kelly, a Mason, by the way, to tour the South and recommend steps to put it on its feet agriculturally. Mr. Kelly had lots of ideas; first of all, that there ought to be a new secret order. It's grown like a healthy child. There are more than eight thousand locals now, with eight hundred thousand members."

"But what does it *do*?" Anne wanted to know. "What are its aims?"

"Plenty—to both questions," he answered. "It's a sort of farmer's school out of school. The idea is to get together

and exchange ideas, to work for better conditions agriculturally, to keep an eye on the farmer's interests in the Government—which it can do, by the way, because it has never
taken a penny's worth of help from public funds. So it's
free to speak its mind. And it's speaking!"

"Ummph," Anne said, biting into a succulent, steaming
ear. "Go on."

"Did you know it was due to the efforts of the Grange
that we enjoy the rural free delivery we have?" Matt demanded. "And governmental experiment stations in agri-
culture? And the protection of the dairy interests?"

"Mmmp," said Anne. She looked up for a moment. "I'm
really learning—painlessly. Don't you want to eat?"

"I don't seem to have the chance. . . . And it was the
Grange that fought for parcel post; the express companies
were against it, of course, but the Grange kept nagging and
jimmying and finally they got the present law in 1912. But
the thing I'm most interested in—aside from soil better-
ment and study of crops—is the cooperative movement.
That's something big. It's just beginning to take hold. And
it's going places."

"You mean—like in China?" Anne asked.

He laughed. "What about here? We have it, too. It was
the Grange that brought over a prominent man from Eng-
land—oh, about sixty years ago—to get it started. It caught
on, slowly but surely, and now more than a quarter of all
the Grange members' stuff is marketed cooperatively. We
buy things that way, too—twine and fertilizer, and feed
and farm supplies. A tremendous saving, when you add it up.
And in some states we have our own insurance companies,
our own gas and oil stations— Say, I'm being gypped out
of my lunch!"

"You can always eat," Anne said, helping herself to another large portion of salad, "but you can't always fill in the gaps of somebody's ignorance like this. . . . Tell me, is this just a men's organization? Don't the women count at all?"

"Don't malign us," Matt said. "We gave women an equal footing from the very first, and a vote. Back in the beginning, that was something. And personally"—he grinned—"I think that's one of the main reasons why we've grown and prospered. Men and women ought to share things. It's crazy to do it any other way. Problems and hardships, as well as success. It's all part of living." He looked across at her. "How'd you like to come to a Grange meeting some evening—see what it is like?"

"I'd like to very much," Anne said, out of her surprise. "The night that you give your talk?"

He laughed. "I wasn't thinking of padding the audience. But if you want to—"

"I do."

"All right, then. That's the fifteenth of next month. You plan to come out here and spend the night. If it's your day for Gansville you could park the Bookmobile in the barn. And if it's not, I could meet you at the bus. There's one from Tilden about six-thirty."

"Your mother—" Anne began.

"Mother will be all right by then," he assured her. "She just has to gather up her strength every once in a while—like this. And if she's not well enough, of course I'd let you know."

Anne sniffed the air. "It smells so good out here—and it looks even better. You must work like a demon. Or does doing it scientifically help?"

He made a grimace. "No matter how scientifically you do it, there's still a lot of plain hard labor connected with it."

"Had you always wanted to be a—that is, to farm?"

"Say it," he commanded. " 'Be a farmer.' There's nothing wrong with that. The people who realize what farming means aren't ashamed of it. . . . Sure, I'd always wanted to manage my own place. Dad built up a pride of the land in me; I went to an aggie college; I took all the courses I thought would help. And now I'm finding out how much there is still to learn. It's a lifetime job."

"Not enough people feel that way, I guess," Anne hazarded.

"More's the pity," he returned. "What I'd like to do after the war is to get some men down here—let 'em see for themselves how the land gives you back more than you put into it if you go at it the right away—and then help them get started on their own. I don't mean to do it by myself; that's one of the things I want the members of the Grange to get back of. If we all did it, we could rehabilitate men and at the same time build up our future stock of farmers. We're going to need them."

"That's a grand idea," Anne said warmly. "How do they feel about it—the other members, I mean?"

"Oh," he shrugged, "everything takes time. I'm not discouraged. If nobody else will tackle it at first, I will. Others will fall in line. Somebody's got to be first and show 'em it can be done. . . . Gosh!" he flung out a hand boyishly. "There are so many things that need tackling like that! I want to get going on the cooperatives, too; I told you that. We haven't begun to dent the market. If I can get enough people to see what it means, we can really go places! That's out of the good things—I hope—to come out of this war."

"You mean—working together?"

"Yes; we've had to, to survive. It hasn't been easy, but it has proved time and again to be the only way. Now if enough of us can only keep that spirit alive, and apply it to daily living, to all the little things as well as to business . . ." He rolled over on his side. "I wanted to get in the war myself the worst way," he said, very low. "At first I was bitter about it; everybody else, it seemed, was getting a chance at—well, adventure and seeing the world and having a whack at the enemy for the sake of democracy. But it was a crazy way to feel. It didn't take me so long to grow up. What I'm doing here isn't very romantic, maybe, looked at that way—a kid's way; but it's as romantic and as glorious as anything a soldier is doing, if I look at it the right way. Helping feed the country; helping feed the soldiers; keeping the land in trust for those who come after me."

Anne said suddenly, "Don't you ever long for a little island with a—a coffeebush and a pecan tree where you could spend the rest of your days?"

He turned to look up at her. "Not unless I'm sick. And I get over it pretty quickly. Lordy, do you? It sounds deadly dull."

"*I* don't want it—no," Anne said vigorously. "I was just thinking—some of the soldiers who come back from the wars might."

"Don't you believe it," Matt said. "Where'd you get that idea?"

"A soldier told me so."

"He was kidding you," Matt pronounced.

"I don't think so.

"Well, then, what's the matter with him? He'd go nuts in six months—or less—sitting on his haunches on his little island, thinking of all he was missing back home: the excitement, the chance to be in on building a new world—"

"But not everyone wants to build a new world," Anne protested. "Some people might like just to go on living in the world-that-was."

"Well, then they'd better wake up. The world-that-was is gone; whether you like it or not, it's gone. There's no use sitting back and moaning about it, either. We helped destroy it; now we've got to start over—and if we don't build a better one than we had, we might just as well crawl back in our caves and let the primordial slime creep over us. Thinking the world-that-was is the only possible kind of world shows a lack of imagination or just plain laziness. Which do *you* think?"

Anne said, perversely, "It's nice to be lazy once in a while."

"Sure. For a time. But the only way you can really enjoy being lazy is remembering what you've done and thinking about what's still to do. That's enjoying your laziness. Otherwise you're just doped."

Anne stood up, shook out her dress. "I'll be doped if I stay here much longer. That Gargantuan lunch and the air and the smell of the trees—" She held out her hand. "Thanks for a lovely hour. I want to say hello and good-by to your mother if she's awake—"

He said, "Do you really feel that way, or do you just like to take the other side of an argument?"

Anne flushed. He cut, always, uncomfortably close to the

core of things. She hadn't been presenting her own side; she had been thinking of Rex and his persuasive talk. But she could hardly say that to Matt.

"Oh," she said at last, "I just wanted to test your convictions."

"I don't think so," he said bluntly. And then, with a grin, "But, for your information, they're unshakable."

CHAPTER EIGHT

THE CAR HUMMED ALONG THE COUNTRY ROAD, AND ANNE thought back over her visit with Matt. It was queer how she always seemed to be giving him the wrong impression. He was so serious—that was it, she decided; he was so serious that he brought out some little perverse streak in her that wanted to shock him out of it. He wanted her to be as purposeful as he was. Well, perhaps she was . . . but she didn't show it. And because he couldn't make her display her seriousness, he didn't believe in it. He was interesting . . . oh, no doubt of that; but a little irritating too.

She couldn't help comparing him and Rex. Not that she approved wholeheartedly of Rex and his ideas, but at least Rex made fun of himself and the world; he didn't insist that everyone be exactly like himself. What had made her bring up Rex's arguments? Just to see what Matt would do—how he'd react? He'd reacted all right. She grinned ruefully to herself. And judged *her* in the reaction.

Well, perhaps that settled the fifteenth. She wondered whether she'd hear from him about it. Not that it mattered really. There were plenty of other things to do. It was just —she faced it honestly—that she wanted him to think favorably of her; and if he let the fifteenth date drop, she'd know that he intended it to be that way.

She pressed her foot impatiently on the accelerator. A

little spurt of speed would do her good; her feelings demanded it. Just a half mile or so. The hum of the motor grew louder; the hot wind fanned her face. Something pent-up and hard inside her felt released with the quickened pace.

She thought, "Maybe if we could take wings and fly when things got us down, we'd be the better for it."

But actual flight wasn't the only release. There were wings for the spirit, too. She carried them with her. For herself, and for all kinds of people. They lay hidden and folded in the books stacked in neat rows behind her. She saw it more and more, with each visit she made. The old woman at Bishop's Fork who had taken wing with *Mary of Scotland* and *A Gathering of Birds.* The work-worn man at Cranley who had straightened and soared away with *Wind, Sand and Stars.* The little boy, timid and defensive, who had taken strength from *Pinocchio* and *Smokey,* and changed before her eyes. The half-grown girl with her sullen face and slouched shoulders and stringy hair who had identified herself with new heroines and seen new horizons in *Madame Curie* and *I Married Adventure* and was making herself over . . . who was even tentatively testing her sprouting wings of the spirit.

Talk of miracles! They took place every day. Doors opened that had been sealed; windows flung wide to let in the sun of knowledge, crutches for the lame, an invisible arm for the wavering, new lands for the hedged, new eyes for the blind. . . .

That brought her back again to Willem Harmsma. She couldn't get him out of her mind. Something that she had read or heard or seen—something long ago in a **magazine**—**somewhere**—kept titillating her brain. But what it was was beyond her; she couldn't bring it to the surface of her consciousness. There was help for him, she knew. She had to find it. It was a kind of challenge. She'd see what she could find at the Library. Maybe something would crop up that would lead her to the right answer. She'd get the girls going on it; perhaps she'd even dare bother Jessica Nichols with it.

What *was* that sound? It was high, eerie, as if carried on the wind. She listened, trying to separate it from the motor's whine. There it came again, a little nearer this time. It was like a child's voice—frightened out of all semblance to itself. A shout for help. Again! . . . She cut the motor; in the sudden stillness it came once more, this time unmistakably a voice raised in hysteria—a desperate cry, frantic with fear.

She leaped down from the truck and shaded her eyes, trying to locate the point from where it came. The river shimmered in the distance, across a field of hay. She began to run. The hay scratched her arms and pricked her ankles. A bee zoomed against her hair and she struck at it, her eyes straining for a spot on the river where a little blob might appear that would tell her the story. She pushed down the slope, slipping and sliding. A boy's straw sun hat lay mutely on the grass. A fishing pole bobbed and eddied out in the stream.

While she stood there, catching her breath from her run across the field, a dark head rose to the surface near the pole. A little boy's face, distorted with fear, stared at her. His mouth opened, a thin hopeless wail this time; an arm raised in appeal. . . . Then he went down. She knew that he would not rise again.

She flung off her shoes, kicking at them with haste; slipped off her skirt. There wasn't time for anything else.

She called "I'm coming! Don't be afraid, I'm coming!" to that empty space of water, and struck out across it.

Her arms moved rhythmically; her legs kicked at the water, propelling her forward with long sure movements. She was a good swimmer . . . there was nothing to fear there. If only she got to him in time! She kept her eyes fastened on that spot near the bobbing pole, memorizing it. But the pole was moving with the current of the stream. How far had it moved? Where was the boy now?

It seemed an endless time till she reached it. She drew a breath and dived downward, eyes searching the bottom. There he floated, a little to the left. She swam over, caught her hand tight in his waistband, and pulled him upward with her. His limp heavy body dragged at her arm; she swam slowly back to shore.

Thank heavens, it wasn't far. She doubted if she could have swum another stroke. His weight dragged at her; she felt as if she barely made any progress at all, and her breath came in gasps. The run across the field, the fright . . . added to the effects of that big lunch. . . . She gave a ragged sob of relief when her feet touched bottom and she staggered over the loose stones, stubbing her toes on a boulder, and laid the little boy on the ground.

His face was a greenish gray; his eyes were closed. The matted dark hair over his forehead gave him a deathlike look. She knelt beside him and listened, feeling for his pulse. The pulse was faint, the heartbeat faint, too, but steady. She rolled him over, folding up her skirt and doubling it over her shoes in an effort to make an improvised, and not very effective, pad under his chest. Now for all the first aid she knew! This wasn't wartime first aid, she thought grimly;

this went back to those faraway days at camp when she had earned her pin and a beautiful scroll as a "lifesaver." But that had been practice on a thoroughly healthy and alive little girl. . . . This was different, terrifyingly different.

She straddled his small body, placed his head to one side, put her hands against his ribs and pressed. Press, count, raise up; press, count, raise up. A small trickle of water came from the side of his mouth with each pressure. The thing was, she knew, to be rhythmic, as rhythmic as the lungs, and to be persistent. Not to give up; not to give up. She said it over and over, under her breath. Press, count, don't give up; press, count, don't give up.

All at once his eyelids flickered and fell again. She could hardly believe that she had really seen it. Then it happened again. Press, count, raise up; press, count, raise up. Suddenly he drew a ragged, gasping breath . . . and she felt her own face crumpling with relief and her body going slack.

He turned his head a fraction and rolled his eyes up at her.

She leaned over, meeting his frightened gaze. "You're going to be all right now," she said soothingly.

Tears rolled down his cheeks. "I feel sick," he said. "I— went down in the water, didn't I?"

She nodded. "Yes, you've had a bad time; but now you're better. Lie still a little; and breathe quietly with me, like this." She steadied her own breathing and made him follow it.

After a while he rolled over. "I could sit up—maybe."

She propped him up against her. "As soon as you feel like it, I'm going to take you home in the car. Do you live near here?"

"Down the road," he said. "It's a white house. I'll show you. My name's Tommy O'Connell," he added. "What's yours?"

They talked for a while, and when she saw him growing restless she knew it was safe to go on. She slipped on shoes and skirt again—the skirt hopelessly wrinkled—and they started across the field together.

Halfway up he stopped. "My pole!" he cried, in a stricken voice. "My pole! It was a new one!"

"It's gone, Tommy," she told him. "I couldn't save you *and* the pole; so I chose you. Wouldn't you have rather had that?"

He looked at her dubiously. "But, gee, it was my new one!"

"I'll get you another," Anne said. "Come along now. They'll be wondering where you are."

"No, they won't," he said. "I said I was goin' fishin'." He added, with a grown-up air, "Fishin' takes time." His deep Irish-blue eyes widened when he looked back from the front seat of the truck and saw the interior full of books. "Gee, are they all yours?" he asked in a voice full of envy. "Have you got any books about trains? Trains and horses?"

"Both," she said. "When we get to your house I'll get them out for you. . . . How many of you are there at home?"

"Oh, there's Mom and Pop, and me . . ."

"Yes?"

"And Bert and Henry and Maureen and Gerry and Brigit and Len and Mary and Jonathan and Stephen and Hannah and Cissy!"

Anne gasped. "Twelve children?"

"Oh—I forgot. An' the baby. He's not got a name yet.

But I think he's going to be called Patrick. There's my house now."

The little white house looked neat and pleasant from a distance. But when they drove up Anne saw the paint peeling from the clapboards, the frayed curtains, the general lack of upkeep.

"No wonder," she thought, "with twelve—no, thirteen—children!"

A tall girl, big-boned, with masses of blond hair skewered high, was carrying out a basket of laundry.

"That's Cissy now!" Tommy cried, clambering down.

Cissy stopped short, seeing the truck. "Tommy O'Connell!" she cried in exasperation. "Where *have* you been? You're all wet."

"I was fishin'," he explained. "I told you I was goin' to catch some fish for you, but my pole got lost—"

She fixed him with her eye. "You fell in the river!"

"Well, *she* pulled me out." He turned toward Anne. "I was full of water. I didn't feel so good. . . . But now I'm hungry."

"I really don't think he's much the worse for his experience," Anne said. "I'm dreadfully sorry we were gone such a time, but I wanted to be sure he could stand the trip back before I started."

Cissy dropped the basket and came forward. "Tommy, I could spank you . . . but I haven't the time," she said vigorously. She wiped her hand on her overall apron and held it out to Anne. "I can never thank you"—her voice lowered. "Tommy's always getting into mischief . . . but he's the dearest of them all. I—I had a feeling somehow I ought to go looking for him, but there was so much to do—" She pushed back a lock of the glistening blond hair, and her full mouth pouted a little. "There's always so much to do! You never get done! I hate it—all of it!"

The air seemed to vibrate around her. Anne looked at her again with heightened interest. She was striking in appearance: cameo-cut features and a long, rounded neck, and the body of a young goddess. Only her eyes were sultry and her mouth drooped with discontent.

"Go and get yourself something to eat, Tommy," she said then. "And you—you must take off your things and let me iron them for you. I've got the irons on now. Come inside while I get you something to put on."

Anne, protesting, still found herself following the tall purposeful girl. The interior of the little house looked as if a whirlwind had struck it. Papers spilled over tables and chairs; piles of dried but unironed laundry lay in uneven heaps on the ironing board and in a carton. The sink was full of dishes from lunch, and above it hung a small mirror. Anne stared at herself with surprised horror.

"Good grief, I had no idea I looked quite like this! It's a wonder I didn't frighten Tommy out of his wits!"

Cissy swept a pile of papers from a chair to the floor. "I can never thank you," she said; her voice was low and husky. She tested an iron with a wet forefinger. "It's ready. You take off your skirt and waist and I'll iron them for you."

Tommy was dispatched to the yard with a piece of bread and butter and two books from the truck.

"I sent some of the others off on a picnic, and Bert's gone to see about a job. Mom's still in bed . . . we have a new baby, you know."

"Tommy told me."

"There's so much to do!" Cissy pushed back her hair again. "I guess I'll never get used to it. The place doesn't always look like this, though. I try to keep it clean, anyhow, even if it isn't neat. But today sort of got me down . . . there was so much laundry, and Mom needing attention, and all the extra diapers."

"Can't some of them help you?"

"I can't stand them underfoot all the time," Cissy said simply. She looked at Anne with a suddenly bleak look. "I don't know how *Mom* stands it, day in and day out. I've almost gone crazy this summer. . . . But maybe that's because I had my heart set on getting away. It was a crazy thing to dream about; I should have known I'd never make it."

"Away?" Anne prodded.

Cissy nodded. "I won a three-hundred-dollar scholarship to Columbia. I want to be a bacteriologist." She said quickly, defensively, "You needn't laugh. I've wanted to ever since I knew what the word meant—even before, I think."

"I'm not laughing," Anne protested. "That's splendid. There's a wonderful field there for girls."

"I know it. That's what makes me so wild. What's three hundred dollars? Just enough to let me dream a minute . . . it's like holding out a glass of water to a person dying of thirst, and then snatching it away again. I'd have to have enough to support me while I was at college. And where's it coming from?" She jerked her arm around the room. "You can see we need every bit we've got. I might as well give up the idea. But I'll tell you one thing"—her voice rose— "I'm not going to stay here all my life! I'd die!"

"You could get a job, perhaps, and earn enough—"

Cissy broke in. "Don't think I haven't thought of it! But how can I? I'm the oldest girl. Mom needs me here. . . . You don't know how I hated to graduate this year, because I knew it meant the end of everything. At least, while I was at school I was out of—all this, and I could imagine something would happen to let me go on. But now . . ."

She shrugged. It was a hopeless, bitter shrug, and wrung Anne's heart.

"You mustn't be so despairing," she said. "Thing's *do* happen."

Cissy's eyes were hot. "To people like you, maybe. Not to me." She leaned across the board, the ironing forgotten for a moment. "Do you know what it's like to wish and wish for something so hard that it hurts you—in here? Of course you don't. You're the kind who can wish for something—and get it."

"That's not true," Anne said quietly. She thought of her determined longing for Claremont, and how Miss Pruitt had dashed her hopes. "I'm sorry if I look so smug. Nobody gets everything he wants."

"Not everything!" Cissy contradicted. "I'm not asking for everything. Just one thing. Just a chance at the work I want to do!" She pushed the iron with sure, hard strokes. "I wouldn't mind how hard I'd have to work at that," she said vehemently. "It's doing this kind of work that I hate. And I'll never like it any better! The boys'll get away. Boys always do. But I won't."

"Yes, you will," Anne said.

Cissy stripped the skirt off the board and held it up. "How?"

Anne said humbly, "I—don't know. I just—feel it."

"When I'm too old to care, probably." Cissy's voice was bitter. "Sometimes I wish I'd never been born, if it's going to mean spending the rest of my life out here—doing things like this. I wouldn't mind if I could see a way out; if I thought it was just for the summer, or just for a year, or even two or three years."

"You have to believe," Anne said. "That's part of it."

Cissy scoffed. "I don't believe in fairies any more. Or in Santa Claus, either. Why try to fool yourself?"

"Didn't you ever hear that faith can move mountains?" Anne demanded.

"Yes, and I don't believe it. I've heard that if you want something badly enough you'll get it, too. I've wanted only one thing for years on end . . . and it's no nearer happening now than it was in the beginning."

CHAPTER NINE

~~~~~~

"RILLA," ANNE ASKED, "WOULD YOU MIND HANDING ME that catalogue on the file?"

Rilla gave it to her and sat down at the opposite desk, leaning her head in her hands.

"What's the matter?" Anne said, looking up. "Don't you feel well?"

"No."

"Have you a pain? Is it indigestion?"

"I wish it were," Rilla said wanly. "I'd know what to do for indigestion."

"Buck up, Rilla; there are others in the same boat," Gertrude Bremmer said heartily. "What you need is to keep busy. You sit and moon too much."

Rilla flared, "I do as much work as anybody! I just haven't my heart in it, that's all. But you needn't insinuate that it doesn't get done."

"Don't get touchy," Gertrude said, with a grin. "I'm not insinuating anything. But if you didn't think about it so much—"

"How can I help thinking about it?" Rilla cried. "It's with me day and night. I haven't heard from Dill in three weeks. That means something—I'm afraid to think *what* it means."

"It means he's busy, or the mails are tied up or lost, or

any one of a dozen things," Gertrude stated. "Keep your head!"

"He used to write every day," Rilla persisted. "I know something's wrong. I can't sleep or eat for thinking of it."

"You mustn't do that, Rilla," Anne put in. "It doesn't help, and it hurts you—and him."

"If only this terrible war were over!" Rilla's voice rose. "It's spoiling everybody's life; it's taking years out of our lives. We're only young once—it's wrong to spend your youth in a war!"

Gertrude eyed her sternly. "Now you go to work!" she ordered. "If you start like that you'll never stop. D'you think any of us like it? D'you think we'd run the world this way if we were asked? Everybody's got a stake in it; we can't wish for things to stop just because our own personal little world would be nicer if they did. The best thing for you to do is to keep cheerful, get your mind on your work—"

"Oh, stop talking about work!" Rilla cried. "I hate this work. I wouldn't care if I never saw the Library again."

"That's helpful," Gertrude said.

"Well, it's true. I want Dill to come back. I want a home of my own."

"That's work, too," Anne said.

"Of course it is. It's the kind I want. This is just marking time, and I don't care who knows it."

"Well, you've certainly told us," Gertrude said. "May I trouble you to reach me the scissors?"

Rilla pushed them across the desk and silence fell. An uneasy silence. It beat in Anne's ears. Rilla's discontent was a tangible thing, poisoning the air. But she couldn't really blame her. Anxiety weighed on Rilla, and she was not one to take waiting philosophically. She was one of those who wanted the world to conform to her own desires and plans; what happened beyond her own little orbit, no matter how serious and breath-taking it might be, did not affect her. Or, rather, she didn't want it to affect her.

Rilla had said so herself. Her work was merely a stop-gap. She wanted Dill to come back, so that she could have a home of her own. Beyond that she didn't care.

How many problems there were, how many unhappy and discontented and troubled hearts! The more you met with people and got to know them, the more you realized it.

Anne laid aside the magazine she had been going over and picked up another. Her eye lit on the table of contents and were suddenly riveted on the words "The Boon of Talking Books." A bell rang in her mind. This must be it! This must be the thing she was searching for, that she had seen long ago but could not remember. Her hand trembled as she turned the pages. She scanned the paragraphs hurriedly.

"Eureka!" she cried, pushing back her chair with a loud scrape.

The others looked up. "What's the matter with *you*?"

"Gertrude, would you mind letting me have your machine for a moment? I want to write a letter. Oh, this is marvelous!"

"I'll let you have the machine if you'll explain the frenzy," Gertrude said good-naturedly, getting up.

"The blind man—this is what I wanted to tell him about —I'll have to get some other information, but it tells you where to write. I suppose, of course, we'd be in the Philadelphia district. I hope I can have something definite the next time I go out."

Rilla said wearily, "It's the heat. I knew it would get her."

Anne danced about impatiently. "I told you about Willem Harmsma, didn't I?"

They shook their heads. "One of your beaux?"

So she told them, in quick, enthusiastic sentences. "He doesn't know Braille, and I *knew* there was something for him; but I couldn't recall what it was or where I had seen it. I'm going to write to the Philadelphia distribution center, and then to the Commission of the Blind in Newark about getting a machine for the records. . . . Oh, I can hardly wait!"

Barely two weeks later she stopped in front of the Harmsma gate. The place looked as deserted as before, but this time she knocked with determination.

After a long wait she heard him calling from inside. "Who's there? What do you want?"

She smiled a little to herself. Her heart was beating hard. It was foolish to feel so frightened, and yet— Perhaps he would think her presumptuous; perhaps he would disdain this help. She could not be sure, and her uncertainty lent a quaver to her voice.

"It's Anne McLane—"

"*Who?*"

"Oh dear," she thought, "he doesn't even remember me!"

"Anne McLane," she repeated, none too surely. "Of the Kenyon County Library. I was here several weeks ago."

She heard him moving about and then the door was opened.

"Why didn't you say so right away?" he demanded.

116

"I've brought you something," she said happily. "Something I think you'll like."

"I don't need any food."

"It's not food—to eat," she said. "If you'll wait a moment I'll bring it. It's in the truck."

He stood rigidly by the door while she went out, and when she returned, staggering a little under the weight, he held the door wide for her. But he was still stiff and unwelcoming.

"How have you been?" she asked, setting her packages on the floor.

"What concern is it of yours?" he asked ungraciously.

She was not daunted. His brusqueness was a protective shell to keep him from being hurt—any more. She knew that now.

"Well, it *is* my concern," she answered cheerfully. "I've thought about you a great deal."

"Nothing better to do?"

"Perhaps . . . but I didn't do it," she answered saucily.

She watched his face. A queer, incredulous expression appeared for a moment, and then was gone; but she felt immensely encouraged. This was a new approach to him. No one had ever talked to him like this before.

She was busy with strings and tape. She had the sensation that he was watching her. The noises, at least, must be intriguing.

"What've you got there—not an animal, I hope? I've got more than enough to look after now."

"No," she said. "Something better. Sit down there in your favorite chair, and just be patient for a minute till I get these undone."

Half reluctantly he obeyed her. He reached for his pipe,

filled and lit it. "I don't know that I care for surprises," he told her.

"That's what I'm going to find out. If you don't, I can take it back with me."

She had the records out now, and she lifted the machine onto a small table. She took a fresh needle from the package and inserted it, laid on record Number 1, started the disk turning, and set the needle down. She was amazed to see how unsteady her hand was, and her breath was coming fast.

A golden voice, deep and intimate and with bell-like clarity, filled the little room. *"Penguin Island,"* it said, "by Anatole France."

And then, " 'In spite of the apparent diversity of the amusements that seem to attract me, my life has but one object. Is is wholly bent upon the accomplishment of one great scheme. I am writing the history of the Penguins. I labor sedulously at this task without allowing myself to be repelled by its frequent difficulties although at times these seem insuperable.' "

Anne could hardly bear to lift her eyes and look across at Willem Harmsma. The voice rose above the thudding of her heart.

" 'Mael, a scion of a royal family of Canbria, was sent in his ninth year to the Abbey of Yvern so that he might there study both sacred and profane learning. At the age of fourteen he renounced his patrimony and took a vow to serve the Lord. His time was divided, according to the rule, between the singing of hymns, the study of grammar, and the meditation of eternal truths.' "

Willem Harmsma sat like a man turned to stone, one hand on the arm of his chair, one hand holding his pipe halfway to his mouth. While Anne looked at him, the deep lines in his face smoothed out a little; his mouth worked; and he suddenly slumped back, twisting his head away from her.

She leaped up, turned off the record. "Are you all right? Mr. Harmsma, are you all right?"

He rasped, "Turn it on . . . turn it on! Dammit, why do you have to cut it off now?"

She put the needle back, and the voice filled the room again. Now she sat quietly, with the lovely liquid sentences rising and falling; with pictures forming in her mind, and the prose of Anatole France transporting her to another world. If it could do this for her, what must it be doing for him? She clasped her hands so tightly that her palms were moist, and she wet her lips.

When, at last, the first side of the record was completed, she turned off the machine and faced him.

"Tell me, what is this?" he demanded. "Tell me what you've done."

It was easy to tell him then. Words poured from her eagerly. "If you like, you can have a new Talking Book every two weeks. Sometimes there are several in one set. They come under government frank, and they can be sent back the same way. I have the catalogues here and I'll read some of the titles to you so that you can choose what you'd prefer to have and in what order, and then I can write the letters for you. . . . It won't be much trouble for you, you see, because they are delivered by parcel post, and they'll come right here to the house and you can return them the same way."

He was silent a moment. "Why did you do this for me?"

"Why—because I wanted to. Because it hurt me to see you longing for books, being unhappy because you couldn't read as you used to. I racked my brain to recall something I'd read or heard . . . but it wasn't until the other week that I ran across an account of Talking Books and knew they were what I had had in mind. But I didn't want to say anything that day because—after all—I didn't know what it was I was trying to find, and I didn't want to raise any false hopes in you until I was sure."

He reached out his hand gropingly, and she put hers into it. "You've opened up a new world for me," he said. "How did you know that I was a fanatic about Anatole France? What made you choose that book as the first one?"

"I—don't know," she confessed. "Having met you, and knowing how you loved stimulating thoughts and beautiful words, it just seemed right. I'm so glad, though, that it *was* the right one to choose!"

He was shaking his head. "I still don't understand it. I don't see why you bothered, why you cared enough to go to this trouble.'"

"Don't *try* to figure it out," she said. "Can't you believe that people do things like that just because they want to—because they're really interested?"

"I haven't found it so."

"Perhaps," Anne said slowly, "you were always self-sufficient. There was no chance for anyone to do anything for you. People are easily frightened off, you know."

He digested that in silence. Then he gave an unexpected chuckle. "You must be pretty hardy, then. I certainly did my best to scare *you* off."

She laughed happily. "I'd hate to have you know how

120

nearly you did scare me off. But I'm glad now I stuck. . . .
You see, I was really terribly thirsty."

"I'd like to go right on listening . . . but I mustn't keep
you here. And I want you to have a list of the books I want.
And you must show me how to use the machine."

She showed him where everything was, had him start and
stop the records himself, impressed on him that he must use
a new needle for each side, and then they settled down to go
over the list.

He was as excited as a child. "I want to read them all!"
he cried. "The old ones that I know, and new ones that
I've never seen."

"Chesterton?" she'd question.

"By all means."

"Conrad?"

"All of Conrad."

"Dickens and Galsworthy and Hardy and Poe, of course."

"Of course."

They chose Marcus Aurelius and William James—"a man
needs to renew his philosophy," Willem Harmsma said
quietly—and Plutarch and Van Loon and Peattie and Mark
Twain; Shaw and Shakespeare and the Greek dramatists;
Lagerlöf and Helen Keller and Saint Exupéry and Hans
Zinnsner. A catholic list, covering all fields, and an exciting
one.

"I'll never get enough," he said. "I'm starved for books;
I'm so greedy for them now I shall get mental indigestion.
. . . But the good part is I can hear them over and over
if I like. Turn back and go over portions I want to study,
or that comfort me or lift me up." Suddenly he faced toward
her, tense and unsmiling. "Maybe you don't know, when

you stopped by that day, how near I was to the end. I was ready to give up."

"Oh, no!" she cried.

"Why not? I didn't have anything to live for." A little of his old brusqueness came back. "I don't have much *now*, for that matter. But there's a ray of hope, at least. A ray of hope that I won't sink down to be completely vegetable. That was what I hated. . . . Having nothing to stir my mind but my own thoughts, and those all bitter."

She opened her mouth to say something, but thought better of it. It was best not to rush him; that would come later.

"I'll send the list off at once," she said instead. "And then the books will start coming, in the order we've marked them. You needn't keep them the full two weeks, of course. Send them back as soon as you've finished." She paused, then said shyly, "And a good summer to you!"

He was out of his chair. "You mean—you won't be coming in again?"

She was touched. "Why, of course, just to see how you're getting on or if there's anything I can do. And if you need help, you can get someone to drop a card to me at the Library."

"God bless you," he said, very low.

She was scarcely out at the truck when she heard the bell-like voice of the reader beginning again. Anne climbed in the driver's seat, laid her head on the wheel, and wept.

CHAPTER TEN

ANNE SAT ON HER BED SURROUNDED BY A HETEROGENE-
ous mass of objects. Her mother, passing in the hall, stuck
her head in the open doorway.

"What *are* you doing, darling? House cleaning?"

"It's time I turned out these drawers—they look like
birds' nests. But what a way to spend an afternoon off!
Where did I get all this junk anyhow?"

"It's always a question," her mother said gaily. "You
can hardly believe you bought it; so it must have been given
to you. . . . The Wednesday Club's having a rummage sale
first thing in the fall. Why don't you get a carton and put
into it whatever you don't want?"

"That's a grand idea!"

"And if you find anything specially nice, you might lay
it aside for the reopening of the Red Cross Shop. They're
always anxious to get some really nice things to sell, you
know."

"I'll do it—*if* I find anything. Right now I'm regarding
most of my belongings with a very jaundiced eye."

"It's just that you don't like the job," her mother said
blithely. "I feel the same way. And, oh, there'll be the
clothing drive in the fall, you know, in case you happen to
get around to your closets!"

"Go away, Mother, before you have me redding up the

whole house! But thanks a million for the suggestions. By the end of the afternoon, I may be able to find my way around this room."

"I'm going to the Twig meeting, dear. If anyone calls—"

"I know—the usual. You'll 'love to come' or you'll 'see if you can do it.' You're just a pushover for committee chairmen."

Her mother said wistfully, "It's the least I can do. Everyone else seems involved in something vital—"

"You do your share, Mother!" Anne said loyally.

"But it isn't just doing your share," Mrs. McLane said. "Not these days. You have to do more than your share. And someone else's." She sighed. "I wish I were young enough to do some of the thrilling things young people are doing now—"

"Like yours truly," Anne put in, stirring a mass of lace and scraps of silk.

Her mother said quietly, "Are you still feeling that way about your work, dear?"

"What way?"

"The way you did in the beginning. I'd thought—"

"I'm not complaining, am I?"

"Not out loud," her mother answered.

Anne got up and paced restlessly across the room. "Well, that's something."

"I don't know that it is. Sometimes it's better to fume and get it out of one's system rather than store it up and brood over it."

Anne wheeled around and laughed. "Mother, you've been reading books on psychology! Run along to your Twig, darling, and I'll beat off all comers."

She had a twinge of real regret as she watched her mother's slight, trim figure disappearing down the walk. Why had she put her off like that? Because she was afraid to speak out? Because she was not sure just how she felt? Because she didn't want to acknowledge her feelings in words? She was baffled by herself. And it was better *not* to talk about it. Lately, at least, she had been able to go along in a routine, plodding fashion, attending to her day's duties, even looking ahead to the next. . . . But if she stopped to wonder about herself, to analyze and probe— who knew what she would find? She was not going to try it. When the summer was safely past, time enough to get out her thoughts and sort them over. Then it would be safe.

Glory, what a weird assortment of odds and ends! A handkerchief case—it was pretty, but she never kept her handkerchiefs in it. Item for the Red Cross. A chiffon head scarf, but a color that didn't go with anything. Where had she acquired it? Oh, yes, that bridge party last year! Red Cross or rummage? Rummage. A trinket box. Likewise. A glove holder. A pottery deer, with one ear nicked. A charm bracelet; and another strung on rubber, from which all the elasticity had departed. A pin with the clasp broken; she had always been intending to have it repaired, but now it didn't seem worth while. . . . What in the world was in this package, so carefully wrapped in tissue paper and tied with ribbon? She couldn't remember, and it had been shoved in the back of the drawer.

Curiously she undid it, and sat staring down at the contents. She spread them out on her lap, and a host of memories came flooding back. The rugs she had woven for her dollhouse! Ye gods, that went back to ancient days! But she could see herself, as clearly as if it were yesterday, sitting absorbed before the small hand loom her father had brought her, while he guided her in the first steps of setting up and then through the breathless moment of weaving the shuttle through the warp. She remembered her thrill of pride as the pattern grew, the ecstatic moment when she had carefully taken off the first little completed rug and held it up for inspection. This was it . . . the blue and pink one. A little ragged and uneven in spots, but it had held together all these years. The next one was better—the yellow and violet one—more evenly spaced and compact. The third, done in black and white, was really good, and the selvage was an achievement. She smiled to herself. When she had finally got that selvage straight it had seemed to her that she had scaled a mountain peak, and her father had been so encouraging.

He had made her the dollhouse as a surprise for her Christmas, that year when she had been so ill, and had furnished it with handmade pieces; but it was the little rugs, he had told her, that had really "set off the rooms." It wasn't till a long time afterward that she realized that the weaving had been a part of her cure, giving her an interest outside herself, teaching her the joy of creation and the pride of accomplishment.

She had gone on to make place mats for the table and lamp rests and a dozen other things. By that time she was well and the loom had served its purpose. Where was it now, she wondered. In a sudden desire to see it she leaped up and began searching through boxes and bags on the closet shelves, and had gone upstairs to the storeroom when the phone rang—rang loud and insistently.

"Darn!" she said, wiping a grimy hand across her cheek, and sneezed. "It would!"

She ran downstairs again. "If it's a committee chairman," she thought grimly, "she isn't going to fare so well at my hands."

"Hello!" she said briskly.

No nonsense in that voice; it was the voice of a busy woman.

"Brrr! You sound like 'No brushes today!'" Rex was laughing. "Icicles are hanging from your ears and your mouth is a hatchet line."

"I ought to hang up on you for that," Anne said. "But it's too true to be funny. Why *will* people call you up when you're in the attic?"

"Because they haven't television yet," he shot back. "It's not just a sadistic desire to raise your blood pressure. And what were you doing in the attic on a day like this?"

"Looking for a loom."

"A what?"

"Loom—l-o-o-m; you know, those things you weave with."

"Yes, yes, I've heard of them. But what for?"

"I wanted to look at it." Anne grinned into the telephone.

"I'll bring you the picture of one," he promised, "if you'll just stay within reach of the telephone after this. It'll be much easier on your temper, and you can look at it as long as you like."

"Did you call up with a reason, by any chance?"

"I did, but your chilly reception practically scared me out of it."

"I thought you were a committee chairman, and I was getting ready to say No."

"Well, forget you ever heard of committee chairmen and get ready to say Yes. I want you to save a week from Thursday evening for something special. Promise?"

"What is it?"

"What would you say to dinner at the Rainbow Room and *Oklahoma* afterward?"

Anne gasped. "Rex! I'd say, 'When did you come into a fortune?'"

"Don't look a gift horse in the mouth. Wouldn't you say, 'Yes, thank you, and how sweet of you to ask me'?"

She laughed. "My very words! Of course you know I'd love it. How shall I manage? Oh, I could take the train directly from Tilden, I suppose."

"I'd meet you at the station, of course."

"It sounds wonderful! What are we celebrating?"

"Oh," he said in his gay, easy voice, "just the fact that I've known you for six months and still like you."

"It seems to be a record of some kind," Anne teased.

"It is. Little you know, girl! I'm amazed at myself. . . . I'll call you a day or two before and get the low-down on trains and so forth. Don't forget our date, now."

"How could I?"

It was really super. Rex always knew how to plan parties, but this was out of the ordinary.

She was thinking happily, "I could wear my shantung suit and a dressy blouse; I could change at the Library before going to the train. And my new flower hat. I'd have to get a pair of gloves, and I *could* do with a summer bag."

She heard the postman open the screen door and throw

the afternoon mail into the vestibule. The storeroom could wait. She ran down the long flight of stairs to see what had come.

There were half a dozen advertisements, a charity appeal, two magazines, and a single letter. It was in an unfamiliar handwriting—strong, black, angular. She puzzled over it before she looked at the postmark. "Gansville, New Jersey." That must be from Matt English, then.

She ripped it open, turned to the signature, and then back again to the beginning. She read slowly, with a leaden heart.

"First of all, Mother wants me to tell you how much she enjoyed those hothouse grapes. Her words are that it was sweet of you to think of her, and they acted as a real tonic. She's up again and quite her usual self, I'm happy to say.

"Which means that we're expecting you on the fifteenth. Mother insists that you plan to spend the night here, and I promise to lock up the Bookmobile so that no harm can come to it. If you're not out on the road that day, there's a train from Tilden at 6:05 which gets to Gansville at 6:40. I'll be there with the station wagon . . . and I guarantee that you will have at least two full hours before you have to listen to 'How to Get the Most Out of Your Land.' Incidentally, that book you were kind enough to bring out was worth its weight in gold. If I can manage to remember even half of what it says I will have them goggle-eyed.

"Let me know your plans; whichever way you arrange it, it will be quite all right. I hope the Grange comes up to your expectations—whatever they are. Till a week from Thursday—Matt English."

A week from Thursday! A week from Thursday! *That*

was the fifteenth! Oh, why did things have to happen this way? It was maddening. She could call it off, of course . . . say she had another date. But that wasn't honest; she had never done a thing like that. She had said she'd love to go with him. But how could she know that she'd have to decide between a Grange meeting and dinner and the theater? It was a mean trick of fate. She bit her lip, trying to decide what to do. It was a losing battle from the start. There was no downing her conscience. She knew she couldn't enjoy the evening with Rex if she broke her date with Matt. . . . It had only been tentative, of course, contingent on his mother's condition. But it was understood that she would come if Mrs. English was well enough.

She'd have to tell Rex. It was a prospect to make her quail. She couldn't blame Rex for being angry and hurt. He'd say, "Why in the world couldn't you have remembered the date in time?" He'd think she was making this up.

She'd better call him now. The longer she waited the more awkward it would be.

She toyed with the idea of writing him a note. It would be so much simpler; she could merely explain and let it go at that. But a letter would take time to reach him, and he really ought to know as soon as possible.

She sighed and called Camp Kilmer, half hoping that the operator would say he was not to be found. Still, she reminded herself sternly, that would merely be putting off a bad moment.

When he answered she said hesitantly, "Are you busy?"

"The Army wouldn't say so, but it's enough for me. Why?"

"I'm sorry to bother you, Rex, but I felt I had to call you about our date."

"Don't worry," he laughed, "I haven't changed my mind. You're still the girl I want to take."

"Don't make it hard," she begged. "I can't go."

"Why not?" There was a distinct change in his voice. "Something better turn up?"

"Oh, you know it's not that! But when you telephoned, I hadn't any idea that a week from Thursday was the fifteenth. You didn't ever mention the date, you see, and I never stopped to figure it out."

"Well, what's the matter with the fifteenth?"

"I—I just remembered or, rather, I was just reminded—that I had promised to go to a meeting that evening."

"With more oomph than the Rainbow Room and *Oklahoma*?"

She said despairingly, "Of course not. It's a Grange meeting."

"A *Grange* meeting?" he repeated incredulously. "For the love of heaven, where?"

"In the country, of course." Some little imp made her add, "To hear a talk on beneficent soil bacteria and plant enzymes."

"Good gosh!" Rex groaned. "You must be crazy! Are you going by yourself?"

"No," she said, "I'm being taken."

"Oh," he said. His voice had cooled perceptibly. "I think I get it."

"I did so want to go with you, Rex," she said miserably. "But I'd really promised, you see—and I didn't realize the date—"

"Well," he said after a chilly little pause, "enjoy yourself. Some people have strange ideas about amusement. Be seeing you . . . I hope."

It was just as bad as she had thought it would be. He was hurt; he didn't understand. She had bungled it, but neither had he made it easy for her. And he hadn't offered to exchange the tickets for another date. Not until then did she realize how much she had been counting on that. Because, if he *had* offered, everything would have been all right. And now it wasn't.

She went back upstairs to the attic, and stared about moodily. She'd wait with writing Matt a note. If she wrote now, she couldn't even begin to simulate any pleasure at the prospect of going to the Grange meeting with him. Why did things have to get mixed up like this? At the moment she wished she had never heard of a Grange.

At dinner that night she said suddenly, "Daddy, you know the dollhouse you made me for Christmas one year?"

"Do I?" he said. "I sported mashed fingers and broken nails for weeks. Not to mention the havoc it wrought with my temper. Even so, looking back, I think I never had a better time. Did a pretty good piece of work at that. It's still intact, isn't it?"

She nodded. "I was looking at it this afternoon. . . . Would you mind very much if I gave it away?"

Her mother cried, "But, Nan dear! What's got into you? Whenever I so much as mentioned it, you flew into a tantrum and wouldn't let me say another word."

"I know," Anne acknowledged. "That was when I was still small."

"I haven't dared bring up the subject since," her mother smiled.

"I wouldn't mind, naturally," her father said. "I've always been proud as punch that you wanted to keep it all these

years. It showed a nice streak of sentiment, I thought. What's up now?"

"I think I've found a worthy successor," Anne said. "I don't know how I'm going to bear parting with it."

She had given up all her childhood toys long ago, including her special family of dolls; but the house was different. That had been peculiarly hers.

"Somebody we know?" her mother asked curiously.

"No," Anne said, and told them about Berta Polachek.

"It came to me while I was looking for the loom," she said. "At first I didn't know why I was looking for it—the loom, I mean—but then I realized that finding the little rugs had set me thinking. Learning to weave might be just what little Berta needs. And then I thought, 'But if she weaves, she ought to have something to weave *for*.' And I faced the fact that I'd have to part with the dollhouse."

"A little involved, but I follow it," her mother said, smiling approval.

"I'm not done yet," Anne warned him. "It's still more involved. Because, though I found the dollhouse, I couldn't find the loom."

"We gave it away, dear, years ago," her mother said. "Don't you remember—Agnes' children wanted one like yours and you gave it to them?"

"If you really want one, I could make one just like it," her father said. "It was a simple little model, but very effective."

Anne jumped up, ran around the table, and put her arms about her father's neck. "Oh, Daddy, *would* you?" she cried. "That's just what I was hoping you'd say!"

He chuckled. "I know your tactics, young lady."

"A simple little model, to use your words," her mother put in, laughing, "but very effective."

"Anyhow, I seem to fall for them every time," Mr. McLane admitted. "Tell me when you'd want this. I think we have enough decent lumber in the cellar; I wouldn't count on getting anything seasoned from the dealer."

She still had to sell Berta herself the idea, as she explained to her father, but she was confident that she could do it.

On her next visit to Freedom Corners, she opened the screen door of Polachek's Grocery Store and found the place as deserted as ever.

"Hi!" Charlie greeted her. "Did you bring *Retreat—Hell!*?"

"No, but we have it."

"Oh gosh, I been wantin' to read that book for weeks! Will you bring it next time?"

"I'll try to. . . . Where is everybody?"

"Mrs. Polly's with Berta. She's bad today. I mean she isn't feelin' so good. I'm tendin' store. . . . Look," he said intensely, "don't you notice anything? Don't you see a difference?"

"Well, I've hardly had time to notice anything, Charlie," Anne protested, laughing.

"But, good gosh, I thought it'd strike you in the eye right away! Everybody else," he said proudly, "saw it right away. It's been workin' good, too."

Anne looked around. The cans, the bins, the kerosene tins . . .

"Oh," she cried, "of course! Why, Charlie, it's wonderful! Did you do it?"

On an overturned case there was a copy of *Suez to Singapore*. Above it hung a large placard, printed in somewhat haphazard, but strikingly black, letters: "You Ought to Read This! It's GOOD! Charlie."

"Yep, I got Mrs. Polly to let me try it; and the very first woman to come in here took the book out. . . . Only it wasn't *Suez to Singapore* then. It was *Leave Her to Heaven.*" He laughed. "She brought it back in two days, and I thought she hadn't read it; but, boy, she knew everything in it! And was she disappointed there wasn't any more by him! I tell you it works fine. People haven't got any—any mind of their own, lots of times. It takes somebody else to tell 'em what to do—even somebody like me. Now they know I like to read . . . and maybe if I've gone to the work of readin' the whole book and I say it's good they'll have a whack at it themselves. They wouldn't try it on their own—oh, no—but let a guy tell 'em it's worth readin' and they're willing to spend some time on it."

"Congratulations," she said. "I had no idea you'd try it so soon."

"I been aimin' to right along, but Mrs. Polly'd never let me. So I told her I didn't see how I could come and watch store any more, and she said, 'Well, go ahead; I guess it won't kill us.' And, what's more, she's sold on the idea now, 'cause I change the book as soon as anybody takes one out; and everybody who's been in has bought somethin'. Don't ask me why!"

"Charlie, perhaps you're going into the wrong profession. Perhaps you ought to take up advertising . . . or selling."

He grinned at her, running his hand through his bright red hair. "Gwan," he said, "you're just kiddin' me. . . . I like to try things out, though, when I have ideas. Gosh, that's the only way to find out what works and what won't!"

Mrs. Polachek came in then and gave Anne a distracted greeting. "I don't know what I do!" she cried. "Berta is so cross today. The heat, it makes her cross. And nothing is right—nothing!"

"Do you mind if I go in and see her a moment?" Anne asked. "There's something I want to ask her."

"Go ahead," Mrs. Polachek said, a little sourly. "But do not blame me if she flies at you. There is nothing to please her today."

Anne went into the little living room opening off the store. Berta was sitting huddled down in a chair, her dress and hair rumpled, her small face screwed into a frown, her lips pouting.

She cast Anne a brief glance, started to brighten, and thought better of it.

"Hello," Anne said. "I've come to see you."

She had made Berta's acquaintance on a previous visit, and had been touched by the small, unhappy figure. They had got along well that time, but this was different. Berta was plainly in a difficult mood.

"What for?" she demanded now, looking up from under her drawn brows.

"Because I want to," Anne said simply. "I want to ask you something. Something very important."

"Don't ask me to be good," Berta's tone was surprisingly mature for a child. " 'Cause I won't be. Mama's always askin' me to be good. Sometimes I will," she added, with a little toss of her head, "and sometimes I won't. And today," she brought out triumphantly, "I won't!"

136

Anne sat down beside her. "I know," she said. "I often feel the same way."

Berta looked at her with interest. "You do?"

"Oh, yes," Anne said matter-of-factly. "Everybody does, I guess, once in a while. But mostly we just feel it; we don't act it."

"I wouldn't act it, either," Berta said suddenly, "if I had something to play with. I'm tired of all my things."

"D'you know," Anne said, "that's just what I came to talk to you about! Berta"—she leaned closer—"you love your dolls, don't you? The ones you showed me last time?"

"Yes," Berta said, still frowning, "but I get tired of them."

"How would you like a house for them to live in?"

"What kind of house?"

"A big house . . . one that you could set here on the table by your chair. Big enough for your mother and father and baby doll. A house with windows and a fireplace and a porch and an elevator—"

She was watching Berta's face. "An *elevator?*" Berta cried. "A real one?"

"Why, of course. You put your doll in it and pull it up to the second floor, or you put her in on the second floor and let her down to the first."

"I want to see it."

"I thought you might. But I had to be sure first. I'll bring it out very soon."

"When?" Berta was to the point.

"Oh, early next week. I have to make a special trip in my car, because I can't get it in the Bookmobile."

"You won't forget it?" Berta demanded.

Anne went home in a happy frame of mind. The first step had been taken. She looked over the dollhouse, seeing it with new eyes and bidding farewell to it. But it was going to someone who needed it now . . . and that was what its destiny should be. There were all kinds of things that she longed to do to it before she took it out. The windows needed washing; the curtains were soiled and a little bedraggled; some of the furniture was coming unglued; the plates on the rack were grimy; a candle was missing from a candlestick; the frame of a tiny picture needed regilding.

But, sternly, she kept herself from refurbishing the house. That should be Berta's pleasure. That should be part of Berta's cure.

Her father drove her out on a Sunday afternoon, and wisely, after he had carried the dollhouse into the Polachek living room, he went out again and waited in the automobile. "Take as long as you like," he said understandingly.

Berta was wide-eyed and unbelieving. She could not really credit her good fortune. She picked things up with careful, loving fingers and put them in place again; she rearranged furniture; she peered into the tiny chest in the bedroom and straightened the vases on the mantelpiece and got out the food from the refrigerator and set it on the kitchen table. She played endlessly with the incredible elevator.

"You won't take it away again, will you?"

"No," said Anne. "It's yours, if you want it."

Berta's eyes were eloquent. "That's what my dolls needed," she said wisely. "A place to live in."

"There are lots of things to do in a house," Anne said. "You know—polishing windows—" she suggested, and waited.

"Yes, and fixing the curtains. Look, I could wash them tomorrow. And maybe Mama could find me a little candle. And I'm going to make washrags and towels for everybody. There aren't any at all!" she said reproachfully.

"I know," Anne said, striving to keep her voice quiet and normal. "And there aren't any rugs on the floors, either. I do think a house looks bare without rugs, don't you?"

"Yes, but I haven't anything for rugs."

Anne said carefully, "You could make some."

"I don't like to sew. I'd make the washrags and towels, but I don't like to sew."

"I mean, you could weave them."

"*Weave* them? I don't know how to weave. What do you weave on?"

"On a loom," Anne said. "I have one I could bring out, and I could show you how. . . . You could make different colors of rugs for each room, with different patterns. You could have winter and summer rugs, and big ones and little ones. And maybe you could make afghans for the baby and spreads for the beds."

"When?" Berta cried. "When? Do you think I *really* could?"

Mrs. Polachek said, when Anne was ready to go, "What do you do? She is different already." Her gloomy nature overcame her. "But if she stays this way after you are gone, I do not know."

"She will," Anne said. "Maybe not all the time. But most of the time. I promise you."

She went out and climbed in beside her father and squeezed his hand. "Hurry up with that loom," she said affectionately. "I have a date to teach Berta how to weave."

CHAPTER ELEVEN

THE MORNING OF THE FIFTEENTH DAWNED WITH OVER-
cast skies and a muggy heat that pressed down and made it
difficult to breathe. Anne looked out of the window gloomily
as she dressed. The shantung suit was out of the question.
. . . But what *did* you wear to a Grange meeting? She
chose the thinnest, coolest thing she owned—a cotton flow-
ered print with a wide woven belt, a dress that had seen
several years' service and had been washed innumerable
times.

"You must take an umbrella, dear," her mother cautioned.
"It's going to rain before the day is over."

Her mother prided herself on being something of a
weather prophet.

Anne made a little face, but, she thought resignedly, an
umbrella wouldn't matter with a costume like this. An umbrella, a cotton print, and her old raffia bag! What an
outfit! She felt far from festive as she started out. And
this was to have been the day for the Rainbow Room and
Oklahoma.

"Have a good time, Nan!" her mother called hopefully.

And Mr. McLane said, "I hope you're taking notes. If
that young chap can tell me how to get more out of my
ground—aside from slugs and ants—I'll be eternally grateful."

140

The bus was jammed with sweaty workers; the air was stifling. Anne was bathed in perspiration by the time she reached the Library and she felt as if a match could touch off her temper. The other members of the staff were in an equally inflammable mood, it developed. Rilla was listless and irritable; Gertrude Bremmer had an attack of asthma; Helen Grant made everyone more uncomfortable by complaining loudly and at frequent intervals of how intolerably hot she was. The phone rang with weary insistence; the desk drawers stuck; the stencil refused to work; and a piece of plaster fell in the stackroom, covering four shelves of closely packed books with fine white dust.

Anne donned an old smock and took dustpan and mop. "You might help, Rilla," she suggested a little tartly. She couldn't ask Gertrude, on account of her asthma, and Helen Grant was busy with the mail.

"Oh, let it lie," Rilla said, her head in her hands. "What's a little more dust? We never use those books anyhow, and the janitor'll be around Saturday."

Anne went off by herself. The smock clung to her bare arms like a woolen blanket, and her moist hair clung to her forehead. Stooping, red-faced and exasperated, she heard Helen Grant's high light voice floating out to her.

"Good gosh, what next! Here's a letter from the Ration Board. They're thinking of cutting down our gas allowance for the next quarter, and meanwhile they want a detailed report of the district we cover, mileage, number of trips—"

Anne hurried into the main room, plaster dust forgotten. "But they *can't* do that!" she cried. "Why, we barely get along now—"

Rilla looked at her cynically. "Who are you to say what a Ration Board can or can't do?" she demanded. "Particularly this Ration Board."

"We'll have to cut out a few stations, I suppose," Gertrude Bremmer said wearily. "Though which ones it will be is a question. They'll all squawk, and you can't blame them."

"Miss Nichols will hate this," Helen commented. "She's just built up the route, and we've been awfully careful."

"Who's going to get out the report?" Gertrude inquired. "I couldn't type a shopping list, with my head. . . . Helen, you'd better get at it." She took the letter, scanned it again. "They want it by Tuesday night for the board meeting."

"I have enough to do," Helen retorted. "What do you think I am—a four-armed wizard? Besides, you know all the dope . . . though why we bother at all is a mystery. They'll cut us anyhow, if that's the way they feel."

"Couldn't we go down to the Board and plead our case?" Anne asked earnestly, pushing the hair off her forehead and leaving a broad white streak.

"Couldn't we move mountains while we're about it?" Rilla inquired. "You do have the quaintest ideas."

"Is this driving *essential*?" Helen Grant mocked. "I'd hate to have to answer twelve gimlet eyes on that one."

"It is," Anne said hotly. "As essential as a dozen other things."

"Don't rouse yourself," Rilla suggested with lazy impudence. "If you have less gas, you have fewer stations to visit. Count your blessings!"

"Well, something *has* to be done," Anne said, with determination and fire in her eye.

"Such as?" Helen Grant inquired mildly. "You make me hotter just to look at you, breathing indignation and righteousness."

"At least I can get the letter ready," Anne said, "if you give me all the information. And it's going to be *some* letter."

"Somebody has to tell Miss Nichols, too," Helen said. "You might like the job, Anne."

She went back to her business of slitting envelopes.

The phone rang. Rilla stared at it a moment, then languidly lifted it from its cradle. She listened in silence, raising her eyebrows at Anne.

"Just another little chore," she mouthed, cupping the telephone. "The Hi-Franc Company librarian wants to know if you can come out today instead of Saturday."

Anne groaned. "She would—on a day like this! What's the matter with Saturday?"

"She says the place will be closed because they're having the painters, and it has to be done over the week end."

Anne stood a moment, irresolute. It was so beastly hot . . . but the atmosphere here at the Library wasn't any too pleasant, either. "All right," she decided, "tell her I'll be there after lunch. I might as well do that as gather up plaster," she added—with a look at Rilla, who blithely ignored it.

Kathleen Marple, the librarian, was apologetic when Anne arrived, hot and tired, at the factory. "I hope you won't put me in your black book for this," she said, "but I didn't see any other way."

She was a tall, thin young woman with burning eyes and a sweet smile.

"Saturday might have been worse," Anne conceded, mopping her face. "How nice that you're going to be furbished up. A coat of paint or two will do wonders in here. It's really a very pleasant room."

"Yes," Miss Marple said eagerly. "I'm so excited. You see, I prevailed on the powers-that-be to let me have the workmen—and that's something like a major triumph these days, with war orders and everything—and then I prevailed on them to let me have the flower and garden show!"

She looked so expectant that Anne rose to the occasion and said, "What flower and garden show?"

"For the factory workers. I've been dying to have it, but I hardly saw my way clear. You know, the management gave plots for victory gardens and we've been encouraging them to do their part and putting out folders and books for them; but I felt the real windup would be a show of their produce and flowers . . . the competitive spirit . . . with pictures in the paper, and ribbons, and cash prizes."

"Wonderful! And has it gone over?"

Miss Marple spread her hands. "My dear, you wouldn't believe it; we already have three hundred entries. We're going to overflow into the corridors; I've arranged to have troughs and trestles all along the hallway leading to this room. And I've had publicity on it, and a photographer's coming to take snapshots of the displays and the winners. *But,*" she said tragically, "I never thought until today that I'd have to have a judge. It just completely escaped me. And I've been telephoning like mad all morning to try and find someone . . . they've all gone away or are too busy or something. I've exhausted my list. Do *you* know of anyone?" she appealed, but not too hopefully.

"You'd want someone prominent, I suppose—a name they knew or had heard about?"

"My dear, I would have liked that in the beginning! But now—I'll take anyone, including the groceryman. Any judge in a crisis. Could you possibly suggest someone I could try? I'd be no end grateful."

The name popped into Anne's mind unbidden. She heard herself saying, "How would you like to have Mrs. Twining?"

Miss Marple's face was fun to watch. Her eyes widened; her mouth opened. "Not—not Mrs. Howard Winthrop Twining?"

Anne nodded. "The same."

"Oh—oh—why, I'd never dream of asking her!"

"But I would," Anne said.

What had got *into* her, she wondered silently.

Kathleen Marple was visibly impressed. "Oh, it would be marvelous," she breathed. "It would make the show. She's known everywhere. . . . But do you think she would come?"

The die was cast, Anne decided; she'd have to make good now; she'd have to ask Mrs. Twining and make her come.

"Call her now," Miss Marple begged. "I must know her answer."

"I'll call her when I go back," Anne said.

That, at least, would give her a little time to select her approach, her words.

"No, no, you must do it now—please," Kathleen Marple said. "There's a phone right here. I'll go out of the room," she added tactfully.

Anne felt cornered. She had met Mrs. Twining only twice since that fateful first meeting, and while relationships were improved they could hardly be called cordial. Mrs. Twining was so domineering, and Anne always thought of so many things she wanted to say and felt she shouldn't say, that their encounters were a bit strained. But Anne had felt an interest on Mrs. Twining's part . . . as if she were trying to fathom this girl who had dared suggest that she buy books, who had dared insinuate that if there were things she thought should be done about the Library she was the one to do them and not Nina Harlowe. Although Mrs. Twining had cut her short on several occasions, she had nevertheless listened with a sort of amazed interest; and once she had even brought the subject back of her own accord—though only to quash an argument Anne had raised.

She was an interesting woman, Anne thought now; interesting but difficult. That is, perhaps she wouldn't be difficult if you knew the right approach to her. So far she hadn't found it.

In fear and trepidation, and only because she knew Kathleen Marple was waiting outside the door in breathless expectation, she called Mrs. Twining's number.

"Perhaps," she thought hopefully, "she's gone away for the summer. Perhaps she's out for the day. Perhap's she's ill."

But she was none of those things. In a surprisingly short time her booming, penetrating voice seemed to fill the Library.

"The connection's very poor, or you're mumbling," she said in her forthright, arrogant manner. "I can scarcely hear a *word* you say. Is it very important?"

"Yes, Mrs. Twining, it is," Anne said brazenly.

Well, it was important to Kathleen Marple and to the workers at Hi-Franc.

"For all the world it sounds as if you were asking me to judge a show."

"I—"

"I haven't a moment now. Come to lunch on Wednesday. That's your day at Harlowe, isn't it?"

"Yes, I—"

"Biddle will call for you at the Library. Nina must come, too. I have something I want to talk to you about. Now don't fail me. Wednesday at one."

And, while Anne still struggled to get in a word, she heard a loud "Good-by" and the connection was broken.

"Is she coming?" Miss Marple burst in to ask.

"I don't know," Anne said. She took out her handkerchief and patted her face, wiped her wet palms. "I'm going there to lunch on Wednesday; that's all I know."

Miss Marple nodded with satisfaction. "Then she'll do it," she decided. "It's as good as settled. I've heard she never asks anyone to lunch unless she likes them. And if she likes you, she'll do it."

"I wish I had your confidence," Anne retorted weakly, but she was excited.

Lunch with Mrs. Twining! It would be an experience worth having, no matter how hard on the nerves.

Changing the book stock was warm work, even with one of the men to help her, and by the time Anne was ready to go she felt as if her head would burst. The heat pressed around her like a tangible thing; she wanted to strike out at it, push it back, draw a lungful of clear, cool air.

She laved her face and wrists in cold water before she made the hot sunny trip back to Kenyon County Library, but by the time she reached there she was bathed in perspiration again. Gertrude Bremmer had gone home on sick leave because of her head; Helen Grant was looking wan and fanning herself desultorily with a magazine; and Rilla sat staring into space, a file of cards spread in disarray over her desk. The plaster dust still lay over the books in the stackroom. Anne wanted to shriek. Would this day never end? She went into the lavatory and doused herself with cold water, but the blood still pounded in her temples.

The air was breathless when she went for the bus. Not a leaf stirred; the sky was a queer grayish yellow. Miraculously there was a vacant seat and she took off her hat and put her head back and closed her eyes. The bus jolted and swayed and her neck snapped; she sat upright again.

Her seatmate, an elderly, plain woman, said companionably, "It's fixin' to storm. When the sky looks like that you can just bet it's fixin' to storm. I hope I get home before it breaks."

"I wish it *would* storm—a storm to end all storms," Anne said petulantly. Her make-up was ruined; her dress was sticking to her uncomfortably. "Anything but this! A person can hardly breathe."

"Oh, no," the woman said. "Oh, no. It'll be a bad one when it comes . . . bad for the crops."

Anne sat silently. It was queer how you could get wrapped up in your own problems, your own comfort. What was to be relief for you would spell ruin for someone else. She felt humbled.

"I'm sorry," she said. "I—I didn't think about the crops."

The woman said, "Well, I guess city folks can't be expected to feel like farmers do about things."

Large fat raindrops were falling when the train reached Gansville. Matt was waiting for her near the tracks and they ran together for the station wagon parked close by.

"But this doesn't mean a thing," he said. "We'll get the works later." When he had her safely stowed, he said, "You were a brick to come. I hope you believe I wouldn't have chosen this weather."

She laughed. "I'm only partly here. The rest of me has melted away somewhere between Tilden and Gansville."

"I'll rush the rest of you home, then, and put you on ice."

Thunder rumbled in the distance and the rain seemed to make the air a bit cooler. But only for a brief while. When it stopped, the mugginess returned.

Mrs. English looked frailer than ever, sitting under the lamplight; but her smile was warm and welcoming. "I'm so glad you could come!" she said eagerly. "Matt will show you the guest room, dear; and you'll want to take a shower before dinner, I know. . . . Didn't you bring your overnight things?"

Anne patted the raffia bag. "In here. I travel light, you see. A shower *would* be heavenly. I'll be ready whenever you say."

She luxuriated under the spray, dusted with powder, did over her hair, renewed her make-up, and came into the living room half an hour later. "Do I look like a new woman? I feel like one."

Mrs. Bartholdy had dinner waiting. Jellied soup and

shrimp salad, tomatoes and vegetables from the garden, an airy lemon pie with a fluffy meringue, and iced coffee.

Anne sighed pleasurably. "Perhaps I'd just better stay here. I might disgrace you by falling asleep at the meeting."

"To the meeting you said you'd go, and to the meeting you're going," Matt said with great firmness. "No crawfishing out at this late date."

"Don't you think you'll have an audience?" she teased.

"Oh, a little thing like the weather won't keep the Grangers away," he retorted. "And they've had fair warning about the subject."

Mrs. Bartholdy was to stay with Mrs. English until they returned, and Matt was to take her home.

"But I'll be up when you come back," Matt's mother said. "I'll want to hear all about it."

Light streamed from the Grange Hall. It was an attractive white building, with large windows and a tower, resembling a church somewhat, and set well back from the road. There were a dozen cars there when they arrived, and Matt and Anne were at once the center of a little group. Anne liked the way everyone greeted Matt.

"Hi there, young fellow!"

"Good evening, Judge Whitaker."

"Only you could have brought me out on a night like this, Matt. You'd better make it good!"

"Thanks, Doctor Cartwright."

The women were friendly and pleasant. Matt had explained that Anne would have to stay outside the hall while the ritual took place, but it wouldn't be long.

"I'll sit in the car and contemplate the stars," she said.

The promise of the rain had withdrawn, and the heat was

more oppressive, by contrast, than it had been before. And, of course, there were no stars—only dark clouds and thick sultry air and a feeling of something about to happen. Thunder still rolled in the hills—now fairly near, now far away—and occasionally a fork of lightning appeared to light the scene with brief intensity.

When it was time for the talk Matt came and got her.

Judge Whitaker introduced him. "We're proud of Matt English," he said. "He has ideas and he's not afraid to try them out. What's more, once he has tried them he's willing —and able—to tell us about them so that we can profit by his success and, possibly, by his mistakes. It's people like Matt English who make our best farmers and our best citizens. Matt always has something to say . . . sometimes we agree with him; sometimes we disagree. But tonight the floor's all his, and we'll hold our horses until he's through." He gave a low chuckly laugh. "If anybody leaves before it's over, we'll know he just can't take it. Matt, go ahead!"

It was as informal as that. Matt stood up, straight and tall, looking very fit in his open-throated white shirt and white trousers, his coppery hair gleaming under the light. He had a straightforward manner and a crystal-clear method of presentation. He talked easily, gesturing occasionally for emphasis, walking up and down the platform as he talked.

He gave a light touch to his words here and there, but underneath was a becoming seriousness. What he had to share with them was real and important to him; he wanted it to be as real and important to them. Matt, she saw in a revealing flash, would never hoard either his knowledge or his good fortune. He had a broader concept of his responsibilities than that.

"The land is not only our heritage," he said, "it is our wealth. If we neglect and dissipate it, we are more than poor—we are fools. We are going to have to produce for ourselves, and for the rest of the world. Science has shown us how we can do it. Why should we be content to follow the timeworn methods that were sufficient unto our forefathers, but are not to us, when we know that we're shirking our duty to the children of the future if we don't make the utmost use of what science has to offer us?"

Anne looked around at the audience. The faces were a study. But Matt had their full attention. The air in the hall was stiflingly close in spite of the open windows. Insects buzzed around the lights, and here and there an absorbed listener swatted absent-mindedly at a mosquito. Farmers in blue jeans and work shirts were here; women with lined faces and workworn hands . . . gentlemen farmers who had driven up in sleek cars, their wives in gay print dresses and modish hair-dos. Storekeepers and grain merchants. The doctor and the lawyer; men with an acre or two in the village; the head of the largest dairy in New Jersey; Mr. Hamilton, who had a ten-thousand-acre estate in the hills and who was planning to turn his farm into a rehabilitation center for returned soldiers. All kinds of people . . . all interested, or ready to be interested . . . a cross section of the country and of democracy.

Anne found herself following Matt's words with a mounting sense of excitement. If he could do that to her, who knew nothing about farming, what could he not do with these people whose main interest, whose livelihood, was on the land? He made it come alive to them—this business of tending the soil so that it returned your work a thousandfold; this task of preparing it to last through the centuries, refreshed and revitalized and ready to yield up its goodness.

Matt put it on a new basis—at least for her. Not as an unequal struggle, an effort to best a clever enemy or a grudging giver, but as a rewarding work with a generous partner. He had figures; he had suggestions; he had new and startling discoveries—put into plain words—at his fingertips. And he made it something that must rouse the best in every man. Anne thought suddenly, and with new meaning, of the Biblical saying "As ye sow, so shall ye reap." It was beautifully true, excitingly true.

When Matt finished she applauded him with spontaneous enthusiasm. Everyone else was applauding too. There were questions flung at him . . . but no arguments. There was nothing to argue here. They wanted to know more. They wanted to know where they could find out more about what he had opened up to them.

Judge Whitaker finally had to put an end to the discussion, with a pleasant little speech of thanks. Afterward a woman got up and announced, with a thrill of pride, that the ticket sale was being highly successful, that they had every chance of selling enough to insure the aim toward which they were pressing—the building of an addition to the Hall.

"And Senator Phillips has agreed to come!" she finished triumphantly. There was a gratifying ripple of appreciation. "He's a big man; there's nobody better in his field, and we feel especially glad that he's consented to take time off from all his duties to come out and talk to us. So please get behind this and sell all the tickets you've been given! It's a wonderful chance for us to go over the top!"

Anne was agreeably surprised. Senator Phillips was a

national figure; he was in great demand as a speaker, and it was quite a feather in the committee's cap to have secured him. She listened with amusement to the hectic discussion of who should be on the welcoming committee, what they should serve for supper, what decorations they would have.

"And now"—Doctor Cartwright rose—"suppose you ladies settle the rest of this some other time. If we let you alone you'll go on all night, and I know from experience that whatever you decide is going to be all right. I came to hear Matt . . . and for the square dances. I've heard Matt, and it's time for the square dances."

Everyone laughed, and rose with a will. Chairs were stacked against the wall; three men disappeared and returned miraculously bearing fiddles, which they tuned up; and a bent old man with lined face and streaming walrus whiskers took up his place as "caller."

Doctor Cartwright came and bowed before Anne. "May I have the pleasure? I've been looking forward to this all evening."

"You'll be sorry," she said. "I know practically nothing about square dances!"

"Follow me and you can't go wrong," he said, and put an expert hand under her elbow.

The fiddle music shrilled and sang, and the thunder rumbled in an incessant accompaniment that was effective and thrilling. Old American tunes punctuated with the caller's droning, "*Grand* right and left. . . . Twirl your partners and a do-si-do!" Laughter rose above the thunder, and the bobbing, quick-stepping figures wove a pattern of light steps on the floor. Anne clasped hands, let go, faced a new partner, bobbed and swayed, rushed in and backed out, exchanging a word or two, a quip and a smile, in a kaleidoscopic succession of steps that left her dizzy and lightheaded. They were all so expert that she *couldn't* go wrong! The hair clung to her neck, her dress billowed gracefully as she whirled from one partner to the next, and her eyes shone with excitement.

"Having a good time?" Matt managed to ask as he passed her.

"No!" she called back. "I'm bored to death—don't I look it?"

Just as the fiddle music rose to a finale, there was a sound that seemed to split their eardrums. Everyone stopped in his tracks.

"Lightning struck—somewhere near here," Matt said.

"Too near for comfort, I'd say."

"Can't have been anything important . . . maybe a tree," someone else said. "Bring on the refreshments; I could drown myself in a barrel of lemonade."

After that first uneasy startled silence, the talk and laughter rose again. Anne was plied with homemade cakes and cookies, delicious lemonade and nut bread, until she protested. The women gathered up the glasses and plates; the men shrugged into their coats; people began straggling reluctantly out of the hall.

Anne said suddenly in a low voice, "Look, Matt!"

He wheeled. "Where?"

"On the stage. Coming from behind the curtain."

"Smoke." It had an ominous sound. "Don't say anything till practically everyone is out of the place. I'll go and investigate."

"I'll go with you."

"You stay here," he said firmly. "I'll be right back."

It seemed that he was gone an agonizingly long time; that people would never cease calling "Good night" and last-minute rejoinders, and go through the outer door. There were perhaps half a dozen left when Matt came running toward them.

"Fire in the storeroom. It's got a good headway."

"Then the lightning struck *here*!"

"And we all stood around like dolts, wondering where!"

"Put in the alarm. . . . Get Edwards to drive in and give it."

"We'll move all the chairs out."

"The records! Save the records!"

"Is anyone down-cellar? . . . Are you sure?"

"Run out and tell the men to move the cars outside the range."

"I'll do it," Anne volunteered.

Men flowed back into the building, carted out equipment. The smoke was tongues of flame now, licking along the curtain, climbing the woodwork, wreathing the windows. It spread with incredible swiftness . . . there was something horrible, something fascinating, about watching its inexorable progress. The men formed a bucket brigade, but it was a hopeless task from the beginning. There weren't enough buckets; the distance to the little lake was too far. It was like pouring drops of water on a raging giant.

"Won't those Volunteers ever get here?"

"It's late—they had to be roused up, and they have to come from Gansville, don't forget."

The lawn was littered with chairs and tables, kitchen utensils, and books when the fire department arrived, clanging their bell, yanking on their coats. But it was a losing battle. Smoke billowed and eddied in a high cloud above and around the building; the white clapboards were consumed in a great bonfire; the windows were red holes in the fire-swept walls.

Anne stood on the grass and watched the destruction.

"It was as dry as a tinderbox—built in 1850, you know."

"Lucky we have insurance."

"A lot of good that'll do. . . . And where do we meet from now on?"

Mrs. Samuels cried, "And Senator Phillips! Where will we have Senator Phillips now?"

They gazed at one another, these women with smoke-blackened faces and wind-blown hair. Tragedy piled on tragedy.

Anne found herself saying, "You could have him in the hall at Gansville."

They stared at her. "What hall?"

"The one above the Library. It isn't fixed up yet; but Miss Newton is dying to have it used, and you could whip it into shape in time. Senator Phillips would be a grand inauguration for it."

"Smart girl!" Matt said approvingly. "I'm glad I brought you along."

"I'm glad I came, Matt."

He couldn't possibly know how deeply she meant that.

CHAPTER TWELVE

~~~~~~

"NEXT," SAID MR. DEVEREAUX, CHAIRMAN OF THE RATION Board, "we'll take up the case of the Kenyon County Library."

He was a portly man, with sagging jowls, puffy cheeks, high color, and slightly protuberant eyes. He looked as if he might burst out of his excellent blue pin-striped suit at any moment. He was one of the leading citizens of Tilden— a retired grain merchant, with various real-estate interests and, in fact, "a finger in most of the pies now baking," as Jessica Nichols had put it.

Anne rose from her chair on the side lines. "I'm here to represent Miss Nichols, the librarian," she said clearly, "at her request."

The eyes of the Board members focused on her. Anne remembered Rilla's flip remark about facing down twelve gimlet eyes. They weren't exactly gimletlike, but they belonged to men who indicated, by their gaze and their attitude, that they would have to be convinced!

"Have you brought the data for which we asked in our letter of—ah—uh"—the chairman reached for a carbon copy in a folder at his side—"the fourteenth?"

"I have everything you asked for," Anne said, "and something else besides."

Mr. Devereaux regarded her suspiciously. "Just the data

158

we mentioned will be sufficient, I believe. We have quite a number of cases to dispose of tonight."

"I won't take long," Anne said.

She felt amazingly calm. Perhaps it had been reckless of her to ask to tackle a matter on which so much depended, but she had felt sure of herself . . . she had wanted to try it. And Jessica Nichols, unable to go herself, had talked things over with her, fortified her with material and arguments, and given her her blessing.

"We can only try," she said philosophically, "and one face-to-face argument is worth ten letters, I've found."

"They've *got* to see it," Anne had cried.

And Jessica Nichols had smiled. "My dear, nothing could mean more to me than the continuance and growth of our service," she said, "but I won't cry over a setback. I've had too many in my life. You learn to go on from there . . . and to build again and over again."

Just the same, Anne felt that the weight of the success or failure of this appeal rested solely on her. And then the fates had given fresh ammunition into her hand. It was the thought of that "secret weapon" resting in her handbag that gave her strength and confidence to face this stern-eyed board.

"You realize, of course," Mr. Devereaux said, with a certain pomposity, folding his hands on his ample front, "that we must make every effort to conserve gasoline and tires. We cannot be discriminating, no matter how much we—as individuals—might desire it. This—ah—uh—duty of ours goes beyond mere personal interest. I hope you will bear that in mind as we ask you questions and ask for facts. It is the facts with which we must deal . . . nothing else."

"I have all the facts with me," said Anne. She held out two neatly typed sheets. "On these you'll see the answers to your questions: the trips we make now, our mileage, our gas consumption. We've worked out our routes with the utmost care; in fact, we've gone over them again and again to see if we couldn't pare a few miles off here, a few there. But, of course, we must consider the demands of our stations somewhat, too—the days they can have us, special requests which must be met, things like that. What we are using now is the absolute minimum. We can't possibly get along with less."

"My dear young lady"—Mr. Devereaux permitted himself a brief smile, somewhat on the vinegary side—"what you say has grown to be a familiar refrain around here. Hasn't it, gentlemen?" The other members of the board nodded solemnly. " 'We can't get along with less.' Everybody says it. Everybody"—he held up a short puffy hand—"undoubtedly means it, as well. But if we listened to them, we should never be able to conserve gasoline and tires . . . which is our ultimate aim. I might say our only aim."

"I know," Anne said slowly. "But there are things we have to conserve, too. Very important things. And that's why we have to ask your help."

Mr. Devereaux looked puzzled. "I'm afraid I don't understand you, Miss—ah—"

"McLane," Anne supplied.

"Miss McLane," he acknowledged, warming to his task. "The plain fact remains, you see, that you are not engaged in a war industry or war work—"

"Oh, yes, we are," she interrupted. "Libraries are continually engaged in war work—war against ignorance and boredom and intolerance and sham and lack of understanding. Every library battles against those enemies. But a county library more than most. If we sink back and don't press our fight, we lose more than the war—we lose the progress of humanity. It takes a long time to wake people up and prod them forward . . . if you don't give them what they need then, you lose them. Forever."

One of the men said, with an embarrassed smile, "She makes out a good case for herself, eh, Devereaux?"

Anne turned to him. "I'm not making out a case for myself," she cried. *"I* can get books when I want them—all I want—at libraries, at bookstores, from friends. I've lived in a pleasant home; I've had a variety of experiences; I've traveled some . . . just as you have. All of you. Our world isn't confined to our dooryard. But for other people it is. They're isolated: men and women on remote farms, children who know only a dozen other children at the country schoolhouse. Books open doors for them; they make them feel they're part of the world. It's a—a kind of freedom we bring them. We can't take it away from them."

She listened to herself almost as if she were another person. Where were the words coming from? Until this moment she had had not the slightest idea what she would say, or how she would say it. But now there was no lack of words. She realized, suddenly, that they were coming from the heart. She was feeling them, and they were pouring forth.

"I wonder if any one of you can imagine what it's like to be blind . . . and to have the only comfort for your bitterness come from books—books that talk?"

She told them about Willem Harmsma.

"Or to be crippled with arthritis, so that you haven't

moved from your chair for twenty years; but to go adventuring through books?"

She told them about Mrs. Anstruther.

"Or to be a young boy who longs to get away from his narrow village and be a civil engineer, and who's preparing by traveling all over the world now—in books?"

She told them about Charlie of Freedom Corners.

She told them, too, briefly, about Minna Hansel, who was learning shorthand at home so that she could get away from a tyrannical father; about Karen Lofstrom, whose drab personality and sense of inferiority were being transformed by a knowledge of dressmaking for herself; about little Mrs. Jensen, who, after thirty years, had browbeaten her husband into building her a box of a home and now was ecstatic over decorating it herself, from books; about Leander Smith, the taciturn old farmer, who had taken up bee-keeping and was setting out an orchard for his bees; about Mrs. Orio, the bewildered young war bride, whose baby was near starvation and who had learned how to care for it through books; about Bennie Yannota, the problem child in a large family, who had become almost a model because he had learned how to make things with his hands—from books.

Case after case swept through her mind; she had not known how many she knew until she began talking about them.

"I could go on as long as you could listen," she said, pulling herself up short. "But I've told you enough to show you what I mean. They're only some of the people we serve. There are thousands of others . . . women who need to read about love and happiness they've never known; men who need to lose themselves, after their wartime worries, in adventures and mysteries; children who yearn for excitement and color and satisfying friends and get them in books. . . . That's why I'm asking you to maintain our allowance."

She drew a deep breath, opened her bag, and pulled out two letters. "And then I want to read you these."

Without waiting for their permission she plunged in.

"Dear Miss Nichols—After you told us what we could do, the other ladies and myself have been working hard to make ourselves a library. I guess you thought we had given up, it's been such a long time, but we had a lot to do before we could even get started.

"We all talked to Mr. Harper, he's a hardware man, and finally he let us have the room above his store . . . or at least we can have it till he rents it. But, by that time, we hope we can make enough money so we can pay him rent and stay. Because we wouldn't want to move now, we have things fixed up so nice. The baker gave us some old bread-and-cake racks that he didn't want, and we painted them and the carpenter made shelves. We painted those, too. And we all scurried around for old chairs, and have half a dozen, with fresh enamel and fresh cushions to match. We made bookracks out of old metal scraps, and we fixed lamp shades and window blinds and made rag rugs.

"We've got everything now but the books. You promised you'd bring us those as soon as we were ready. So please come and see how fine we are. We can never thank you for your encouragement. We'd like some love stories, please, and some books about fine people, and some on gardening, and some cookbooks with new recipes in them. We will wait for you, so let us know the day you can come and we will make it a party.

"Mrs. Eliza Farnham, Mastersburg, New Jersey."

Anne looked up briefly as she finished. "That's one; here's the other," she said.

"Dear Miss Nichols—I've tried and tried to find a place for our library, but there's no building suitable. So I've decided that we must not wait any longer. My daughter has married and gone away to live, so I can turn her room into a library. I'll fix it up and, since I'm always at home, I can take charge, if you'll just show me how you want things kept. There are twelve families here who are longing for books, and this seems the best way to start. Maybe we will grow, but anyhow I know we twelve families need a library now. I'm happy that I can do this much to help. Let me hear from you soon, and please accept my regards.

"Mrs. Helga Larson, Norwell, New Jersey."

Anne folded the sheet carefully.

"Norwell?" said Mr. Devereaux. "Where is it? I never heard of it."

"Not many people have," Anne replied. "It's a little factory community about twenty miles south of Kinsbury. Rather barren, flat country, very uninteresting. A factory, and a group of houses and a store or two. That's all . . . absolutely all."

She straightened. "And those two letters," she said firmly, before her courage gave way, "are why I am asking you for *additional* gas. We want those stations to be established. There's a need for them. I hope I have made you see how much need there is for them."

She stood, then, quietly. She had done all she could. The

men looked from one to another, and at Mr. Devereaux.

One of them said, "I'd say give it to her, Devereaux. If you don't now, she'll talk us down in the end. Boy, what a salesman she'd make!"

Anne laughed in shaky relief.

Mr. Devereaux said, "Not so fast, Howard, not so fast. Miss McLane, we appreciate your coming and placing this information before us. Please be assured that we'll take what you have said under advisement, and let you know at the—ah, earliest opportunity."

Anne said, "Thank you very much. And when would that be?"

He blinked a little, but his pomposity seemed to relax a trifle. "Matters have to go through regular channels, of course," he said. "But if you will furnish us with data on the extra mileage, I think we can say—"

He looked for assistance at the other men, and the one called Howard said jovially, "Make it day after tomorrow. And, young lady, if you ever get tired of the work you're in, come and see me. I could use you in my business."

Mr. Devereaux looked reprovingly at Howard. "Miss McLane," he said, "you do realize, I'm sure, that the Ration Board is ever willing—nay, eager—to assist in worth-while and *necessary* undertakings."

"I do," said Anne demurely. "And I am so grateful. Thank you—for myself, and particularly for Miss Nichols and the people whom you have helped."

"Harrumph," said Mr. Devereaux. "Well, I think we shall have to proceed to the next case. It is a busy evening."

It was a real triumph. Not for herself, Anne knew, but for the Kenyon County Library and the work it was doing.

She spent the night with Gertrude Bremmer, who had to hear all the details so that she could relay them to an overjoyed Miss Nichols when she went to visit her.

Anne set out next morning with a high heart for her luncheon date with Mrs. Twining.

Nina Lonsdale was grim as they sat together in the ancient Twining Cadillac, with a portly Biddle at the wheel. "It will be a perfectly magnificent luncheon," she said gloomily, "and I won't enjoy a bite of it. I'd rather have a sandwich and a thermos of coffee by myself at the Library."

"Why?" Anne asked, smiling a little at the miserable Nina.

"Oh, I like to eat in peace. And she keeps firing questions at me when I'm just about to swallow, or brings up something that I can't argue without letting things get cold, and then just as I'm about to take up my fork again she says, 'Eat your lunch, Nina; you're so slow, and the next course is waiting.' I feel—baffled, and it always gives me indigestion."

"Well, this time you just eat and let me talk. I had a large breakfast at Gertrude's, and I won't mind. . . . Tell me about the place, Nina."

But Nina shook her head. "No," she said. "You'll have to wait and see for yourself. I couldn't begin to do it justice."

They rolled up a white gravel driveway between matching cedars. Emerald lawns sloped away on either side, and there were stables and barns in the distance. The house was mellow brick of Georgian design, with white portico and trim and twelve-paned windows glistening in the sunlight.

An elderly maid, in a surprisingly old-fashioned uniform,

opened the door. "Mrs. Twining will be in directly," she said. "She said you were to wait in the little parlor."

The little parlor was Victorian in the extreme. Carved walnut furniture and low tufted chairs, draped curtains and heavy carpet and a handsome embroidered bell pull. In a corner was a glass-doored cupboard with some beautiful fans displayed on the shelves.

"That one," Nina said, pointing, "belonged to the Empress Eugénie, and this one with the mother-of-pearl handle was given her by some Italian prince, and this one belonged to a Chinese lady of the something-or-other dynasty—I never can keep them straight."

Anne laughed. "You sound practically like a guide."

"Heavens, I've heard it often enough. And I'll hear it again today. Wait till she gets started on her laces. And the history of the silver pomanders will take her all afternoon."

"They'll have to wait then. I have to get back to Tilden."

"You'll stay until she's finished," Nina said. "Don't I know? She loves to tell about them and you're a brand-new audience. *I* shall probably manage to slip away unnoticed . . . if I'm lucky."

"Ah, here you are!" Mrs. Twining's voice preceded her ample self through the doorway. "You're prompt. . . . But, of course, why shouldn't you be," she demanded, more or less of herself, "since Biddle fetched you?" She gave Nina a brisk nod, and pumped Anne's hand up and down twice, briefly, then let it drop. "Let's go in to lunch at once. I'm famished. Been tramping over the place all morning—my superintendent's leaving next month, more fool he!"

She glanced down complacently at her muddied ghillies, leaving spots of brown earth on the heavy purple carpet;

tucked in a wisp of hair, which promptly escaped again; pushed her hat down more firmly on her head; adjusted her somewhat rumpled jacket; and stalked ahead of them into the dining room.

A massive refectory table was set for three at one end. Anne's appreciative eye took in the cobwebby lace doilies, the Venetian glass and pottery, and the fragile silver.

Mrs. Twining pulled up her chair and said, turning to Anne, "Now, tell me, for heaven's sake, what you were trying to say over the telephone the other day."

Another maid, in equally old-fashioned uniform, set down covered soup dishes, from which, when the lids were removed, a heavenly fragrance arose.

Anne plunged in; it seemed the only approach with Mrs. Twining. "I was telephoning from the Hi-Franc Company to ask if you'd be the judge at their flower show."

Mrs. Twining broke a roll, piled a large lump of butter on half of it, and popped it into her mouth. "Hi-Franc? What's that, in the name of sense?"

"It's a roller-bearing company," Anne said. "They're working three shifts on war orders. They have a tremendous colony of workers in the town, and a trailer camp outside; and they draw people from all over the state. The librarian is planning a flower and garden show to display what the workers have grown on their victory plots."

"And what made her think I'd be the judge?" Mrs. Twining demanded.

Anne realized what Nina meant . . . she had just been about to swallow. She gulped hastily, "Miss Marple didn't think of asking you. *I* did."

"Why?" It sounded like a bullet hitting a target.

"Because I knew your reputation in judging circles, and I wanted them to have the stimulus of your presence."

Mrs. Twining glanced at her sharply, but said nothing.

Anne continued, "It would be a tremendous boost for the show. Miss Marple is thrilled over the mere prospect. *She* was afraid to ask you."

"But you weren't?"

Anne didn't stop to analyze that remark. "No," she said candidly.

"Why not? I'm a very busy woman. A *very* busy woman."

"I know," Anne said. "That's why I felt safe in asking you. Busy people are the ones who know how to budget their time; they're the people who get things done."

Mrs. Twining said, "Nina, eat your soup. You're so thin you make me uncomfortable. And put butter on your roll. Good heavens, haven't you *touched* it yet?"

Nina began, "I haven't—"

"Don't tell me you haven't any appetite," Mrs. Twining interrupted. "You say that every time. Just eat. I'll do the talking. I have a great deal to say to you, and I've a meeting at three. Now, first of all, have you had the shelves painted?"

Nina put down the roll she had dutifully picked up. "No, Mrs. Twining."

"Why not? They're in a disgraceful state; they make the whole room look shabby."

"I know, but we just haven't the money. I thought perhaps later, if I could manage the time, I might do them myself."

"Nonsense. As for money, surely you haven't spent the whole budget this year?"

"No, but what's left has to go for repairs—real repairs, I mean, like the roof and new gutters—and the rest is for books."

Mrs. Twining snorted. "You spend more and more for books. I think you'd let the roof fall in if it meant you could buy another dictionary."

Nina's chin lifted a trifle. "I almost would! After all, that's what a library is for . . . to have the kind of books that people need. And we haven't nearly enough of them. Why, just the other day, Terry Brunson was in—"

"Well, Nina, you needn't feel badly just because you can't supply every book a child wants. After all, you're not the New York Public."

"But don't you see—" Nina began desperately. She crumbled a piece of roll between nervous fingers. "We need *books* . . . not paint for the shelves, and new andirons for the fireplace, and new glass curtains for the door, and new black frames for our lithographs. . . . I wish we could have those things, too; but since there isn't money for both, it just has to be books. Dictionaries, and reference books and biographies, and encyclopedias—why, our encyclopedia is so out-of-date it makes me ashamed—"

Mrs. Twining said, "I thought *I* was to do the talking."

Nina's lips trembled. "I'm sorry—no, Mrs. Twining, I'm *not* sorry," she said surprisingly. "I had to say it. I've wanted to for a long time."

Mrs. Twining waited till the maid had taken away the soup and brought plates of lobster salad and little green peas. Then she said, with chilling deliberateness, "And what else have you on your mind, Nina?"

The little librarian's eyes looked enormous, and her face was pale with emotion—and a new kind of strength. "Do you really want to know, Mrs. Twining?"

"I should not have asked otherwise," Mrs. Twining replied icily.

She kept her gaze fastened on Nina, and Anne thought swiftly of the elephant and the mouse. Nina was the mouse . . . but not all courage was in the elephant.

"I've thought so many times," Nina said in a voice breathless with her own daring, "so many times—how easy it would be for you to help me get the things the Library needs. If you spoke to the other board members, if you used your influence for us—you *have* influence with them; they do anything you say—if you made them see how greatly we need books instead of . . . andirons, for instance—"

"Go on," Mrs Twining commanded.

"And then"—Nina gulped, but she did go on—"if they wouldn't see it, anyhow, I've thought how just one of those fans you have in there"—she gestured swiftly toward the little parlor—"the one perhaps that Empress Eugénie had carried . . . how that would mean a whole new set of science books, or a new Britannica."

Her voice trailed off; suddenly she looked sick, stricken.

Mrs. Twining said, softly for her, "You know, Nina, that I could have your job for this."

Nina nodded. "I know," she whispered.

Mrs. Twining let a long pause settle on the table; it weighted the room. Nina's breath was coming in rapid little flutters, and Anne wanted to push back her chair, to shout, to make a noise—anything to stab through that cruel moment.

"But," Mrs. Twining said then, "but I'll not. I'll not have your job for that, Nina."

Nina's head jerked up; a slow flush stained her cheeks.

"No," said Mrs. Twining, evidently enjoying her role, "I think, instead, I'll ask for an advance in salary for you. You've always struck me as such a worm, Nina. No spunk, no grit, no—sass, as we used to say when I was a girl. It has always rubbed me the wrong way. I've tried to rouse you a hundred times; once in a while I'd think I had struck a spark, and then you'd subside again, like a little scared rabbit, into 'Yes, Mrs. Twining.' . . . 'No, Mrs. Twining.' At last I seem to have discovered that you're commendably human. Eat your lobster."

Nina apparently could not have spoken if she had wanted to. She pecked frantically at her lobster; the peas slid off her trembling fork.

"So you think a fan would set up your library, eh?" Mrs. Twining mused. She tucked in the recalcitrant wisp of hair again and pushed her hat lower on her forehead. "I never thought of it that way. I've more fans than I know what to do with, anyhow. After lunch—if you ever finish, Nina—you may pick one out . . . but *not* the one that the Italian count gave me; that was my first summer abroad, and he was very romantic . . . and I'll sell it and you may have the proceeds to do with as you please."

Suddenly she laughed; it was a terrifying sound in the very quiet room. It echoed and boomed and beat upon Anne's ears.

"I'll wager the Empress Eugénie never thought that one of her fans would turn into a Britannica . . . and *I* never thought that I'd be the one to do it."

Afterward she turned to Anne. "Has Nina told you about my collections?"

"Yes," said Anne, "she has. She was just beginning to show me some of the things when you came in."

"Well, Nina's not the proper person to show you," Mrs. Twining said. "I always thought she hadn't enough appreciation of them . . . now I know it. I'll show them to you myself."

She began to spoon vigorously into the strawberry mousse. "Needs more sugar," she commented, but it did not seem to lessen her pleasure in it. "Do you collect anything? Everyone should."

Anne said, "Only little animals. My father started it when he went away on trips and would bring me a different animal each time. But it's been a long time since I've added anything to it. If I had money—"

She bit her lip. It had slipped out.

Mrs. Twining evidently misunderstood her. "It needn't take much money, but you *should* keep up collecting. After all, what you spend on a dress or even a pair of stockings could perhaps give you a new, interesting piece."

Anne took a deep breath. "No," she said, "that isn't what I meant. If I had money I should go in for an entirely different kind of collecting."

Mrs. Twining looked up. "What do you mean?"

"I'd collect—people," Anne answered simply.

"People? People? Wouldn't that be difficult—or are you trying to be funny?"

It was Anne's turn to be frightened, but somehow she couldn't be. "I'm not trying to be funny; that much I know, Mrs. Twining. Though, of course, collecting people might be difficult. But, oh, what fun it would be! To know that you'd had a hand in giving them happiness, or a chance to become whole personalities, or to develop their talents, or to get away from an intolerable situation— You'd hardly know where to stop!"

Mrs. Twining was looking at her with a peculiar gaze; it made Anne uncomfortably aware of how far she had trespassed on Mrs. Twining's hospitality and, possibly, good nature. But there was no turning back now. It was a subject she had thought about so often—daydreaming of what she would do if the miracle happened and she were wealthy, with money to spend on whatever she pleased—that it had slipped out. And at least she had Mrs. Twining's reluctant interest.

"You're like a great many people," Mrs. Twining said, a bit tartly. "You believe that money solves everything. It doesn't. It merely makes more problems. Because you happen to have money you can't settle the world."

"No," said Anne, "but you could help. If you saw somebody who needed a lift, you could give it to him. Even this summer, in the few months I've been going about here, I've seen half a dozen cases where I'd—I'd give my soul to be able to help! Old Mrs. Anstruther, for instance, who's so crippled with arthritis that she can hardly walk; I'd love to be able to send her to Tucson . . . maybe it wouldn't cure her, because it's too late, but she'd have a happy winter; she'd get away from her crowded little house and her nagging daughter-in-law. And Willem Harmsma—I'd get him to go to Morristown and get a Seeing Eye Dog . . . he thinks he can't afford it; but if you could make him go, make him realize how much freer and more independent he would be, he'd soon pay you back. And Cissy O'Connell—"

She broke off. She was really being impossible.

Mrs. Twining snapped, "What about Cissy O'Connell, whoever she is?"

Anne said suddenly, "Did you ever wish for something so hard that it was like a physical pain . . . something that was just out of reach and that made you feel—frustrated because you couldn't grasp it? Something you wanted to do and fate wouldn't let you? . . . But, of course, you haven't."

"Why not?" Mrs. Twining said belligerently. "What do you think my life has been—a bed of roses?"

"No," Anne admitted, "but if you wanted to do something, you could just go ahead."

"Not at all. When I was a girl—" Mrs. Twining drew a deep breath, and her face fell into hard lines. "When I was a girl I wanted to be a doctor. It wasn't done in my day. Women didn't become doctors . . . anyhow, not the women of my family. My father put his foot down. I threatened to run away; but he said, quite rightly, 'And if you did, what would you live on? And where would you go? I should write to every school, every college, forbidding your entrance; refusing to pay your tuition.' I twisted and turned in every direction I could think of, but it was like butting your head against a wall. After a time I gave up . . . and married. But I never got over that longing. If I weren't a fool I'd go out now and enter medical school; I have the brains, the strength. Only, after the years go by, you lose the impetus. A kind of inertia sets in. You have to do things like that when you're young—or you never do them."

Anne nodded excitedly. She hadn't time to ponder on the amazing fact that Mrs. Twining was human . . . that she had felt ambition and frustration, too. She only knew that, with this confession, she had been given a miraculous advantage to press.

"That's the way Cissy feels, I think," she said. "If you wanted to be a doctor so passionately, you'll know how Cissy feels about wanting to be a bacteriologist. She's afraid, you see. Afraid that if she doesn't get to do it now she'll never get to do it."

Mrs. Twining had withdrawn a little, as if she regretted her outburst. "Matters are different nowadays," she said. "There are scholarships."

"Cissy has one. A three-hundred-dollar one. But she can't use it."

"Why not?"

No matter how prepared you thought you were for Mrs. Twining's questions, they hit you with the force of a rifle-shot.

Anne said, "They have twelve children—"

"Good heavens! In these days!"

"And a new baby makes thirteen. Cissy's the oldest girl. She has to stay at home—or thinks she does. And even if she could get away there wouldn't be enough money."

"What does the father do?"

"He works for the railroad now, but Cissy said his ambition was to buy a really good farm and work it."

"Has he had experience?"

"He was raised on one, and he used to manage a small estate before he married."

Mrs. Twining's eyes narrowed. "There's a nice house here; we could put in extra beds—but, still, they probably have all their furniture. If he's any good at all it seems providential—" She was thinking out loud. Anne held her breath. "I could use several of the boys on the place, and the girls too. There's a good school near by." She wheeled suddenly to Anne. "I'd like to meet this Cissy of yours. What's she like? No, don't tell me. I form my own opinions. Too many girls nowadays have an idea for a career, but no stick-to-itiveness. If I were to—" She broke off; and began again firmly, jutting out her chin. "She'd have to be good . . . *very* good. If she disappointed me, I'd hold you responsible."

Anne said happily, "She won't disappoint you. Not Cissy."

Mrs. Twining pushed back her chair. "We'll not talk about it any more. If I decide to do anything, I'll get in touch with you. . . . Now I want to show you my collections."

Anne said, with a firmness she did not feel, "I really must go back with Nina, Mrs. Twining. I have a full afternoon."

Mrs. Twining's face fell; she looked oddly like a child whose lollipop has been snatched from her.

In that instant Anne was sorry for her. "Perhaps," she said impulsively, "you'll let me come some other time?"

"I shall expect it," said Mrs. Twining. "When you come to Harlowe again. Nina, you too."

Nina started toward the door.

"Come back and choose your fan! Surely you're not going without your fan!"

Nina's face worked. "Oh, really, Mrs. Twining, I couldn't —after all—"

"After all, you said it; now you'll abide by it."

Nina, looking more frightened than ever, straightened her shoulders, like a convict being led to the gallows.

"You seem to have had your eye on the Eugénie one. A

good one to have your eye on, I must say." She opened the case, lifted it out gently, and laid it aside. "And what about this one? It's one that was said to have been carried by Mrs. Washington, but I doubt it; I never could authenticate it. Still, it ought to bring a good price. And I'm tired of it. We'll put that one aside, too. But, Nina—"

"Yes, Mrs. Twining?"

"I warn you; this one *must* go for painting the bookshelves. Then, if there's anything left, you may spend it for books. Is that understood?"

As they were finally starting away, Anne asked, "About the show, Mrs. Twining?"

"What about it?"

"You haven't said whether you'd judge it for them."

"Of course I will! I didn't refuse outright, did I? I thought that was all settled. Send me the date, the name of the librarian, and a list of entries; so I'm somewhat prepared. I hope it won't take all afternoon. And I shall want a cup of tea. It's arduous work, and I insist on a cup of tea."

"I'm sure Miss Marple will be delighted to see that you have it."

Biddle took them back to the Library.

Nina settled in a corner of the fawn upholstery and closed her eyes. "I feel as if I'd been through the war."

"You must keep it up now, Nina. She loved it! I told you she was like Miss Partridge!"

"I should never have done it if it hadn't been for you."

"Don't be silly! It was bound to happen someday. People like that drive you till you finally turn on them . . . and then you find that that's exactly what they've been wanting you to do. It's queer."

"I feel sorry for that Cissy. Her life won't be her own."

Anne laughed confidently. "You don't know Cissy! They may fight at first, but she'll end by having Mrs. Twining eating out of her hand."

Nina waved her hands weakly. "Well, perhaps. . . . I'm sure I'm not the one to doubt it. I was never so surprised in my life as I was at myself." She grinned at Anne. "But it's terribly wearing!"

CHAPTER THIRTEEN

THE WEATHER WAS PERFECT FOR ADA HOWLAND'S PARTY. A clear sky, with theatrically spaced small white clouds; new-washed air fanned by a faint breeze; the lawns freshly clipped, and the flower beds blazing in splendor.

"I *do* have the most amazing luck," Ada Howland said, enveloping Anne in a capacious hug. "If I ever decide to give anything, or go anywhere, the weatherman always cooperates. It's a gift!" She laughed happily. "My dear, how sweet you look! You're going to *make* the party!"

She held Anne off and looked at her fondly. "I tried to look festive and at the same time—serviceable," Anne returned "What can I do to help?"

"Not a thing at the moment, darling. Except float around and talk to all the old gentlemen and make them feel gay. Later on I shall want you to be nice to the 'talent.' "

"Oh, did they all come?"

"Every one, bless their hearts! I'm so excited! They're in the guesthouse now, making up and resting. I'll introduce you, and you must look after them till they go on." She gave Anne's arm a squeeze. "You're such a treasure. I don't know what I would do without you!"

That was an exaggeration and Anne knew it, for Ada Howland was entirely capable of carrying on alone; but she made it sound sincere. Ada looked radiant; her golden hair had been newly glorified and was topped by a magnificent black hat of great circumference, adorned with nodding roses and a spray of lilacs that bobbed when she talked. Chiffon half-sleeves fell over her white arms, and her wrists were hidden by a dozen bangles that clanked and chimed with every movement. She wore a batiked dress in which all the colors of the rainbow swirled dizzily.

"It's a little tight in spots—I *have* put on weight here in the country. But isn't it sweet? I could never bear to part with it. And it's just right for this sort of thing. Colorful, you know, and—easily seen. If I'm to be mistress of ceremonies, I have to be seen!"

Anne's eyes swept the grounds. There was no doubt about it—Ada Howland was a wonderful organizer. "Everything looks marvelous!" she breathed. "How did you ever do it?"

"Doesn't it look idyllic? Ah, we had such happy times here!"

She had persuaded the new owners of her former estate, who had gone away for the summer, to let her have the place for her party, and they had agreed.

Anne thought, "It would be hard to refuse Ada Howland anything once she had made up her mind to have it."

With the setting assured, Ada had gone to work in earnest. Posters, advertising, carpenters setting up booths and Scouts decorating them; the women inveigled into baking cakes and making candy and aprons and potholders and baby sacques . . . the florists cajoled into donating corsages, the restaurants into giving ice cream, the local merchants browbeaten into offering merchandise to be sold. And, keeping up with her personal triumphs, a constant barrage of ticket selling.

The library door had a sign on it: "Closed—Just for To-day! Come to Our Party and Help Us Grow! Hilltop Vista —Admission Fifty Cents!"

And they came. By ones and twos. Groups of children. Women in farm carts. Women in sleek automobiles. Little girls wheeling prams. Elderly gentlemen with canes. Look-ing expectant, doubtful, or surprised. But coming.

Ada Howland had a word for each of them. "There's some delicious fudge over there, Gloria—only ten cents a bag. You'd better hurry! . . . Oh, Mr. Whipple, how nice! Would you mind helping Mrs. Gentian fix the flag? You *know* all about those things! . . . That cake you sent looks simply heavenly, Emaline! It's going to be auctioned off. Nobody could afford to *pay* what it's really worth! . . . *Dear* Mrs. Garland, let Freddie carry a chair over in the shade for you and you won't have to stir; everyone will simply come and talk to *you*!"

"Ada Howland has the magic touch," Anne thought, watching her.

Women preened a little; men became courtly and gallant; little boys fell over themselves dragging boxes and chairs wherever she wanted them; and the little girls followed her about, openmouthed and adoring. She was having such a good time herself that everyone else had a good time. Old Mr. Cranbury bought a pair of baby's booties simply be-cause she asked him to, and then returned them to the table. Mrs. Carmichael, who was muttering that she was dead on her feet, melted at Ada's appeal and said she would be glad to wash the ice-cream dishes. Haughty Mrs. Seibold offered to tell fortunes if they'd fix her up a tent, and in the midst of everything little Jed Taylor fell into the fish-pool.

It would have taken only two minutes for Mrs. Taylor to go off into a fine set of hysterics and Jed into a bad case of weeping; but Ada Howland snatched a towel from one of the tables and an ice-cream cone from another, and, enveloping Jed in the towel, she expertly popped the cone into his hand.

"Darling, I do hope you didn't scare the fishes! That was the most beautiful dive I ever saw. Look how proud Mother is of you!"

She fixed Mrs. Taylor with a compelling eye, and Mrs. Taylor promptly smiled.

When the booths were growing bare and people were beginning to mill around a little aimlessly, Ada Howland's sense of timing came to the fore. "Listen to me, everybody!" she called in her clear, penetrating voice. And they all turned and listened. "Bring your chairs over here, all of you, and sit where you can see the platform. I've a very special treat in store for you. This is the part of the afternoon you've all been waiting for. You've been so dear and generous; now you shall have your reward. And I can never, never be grateful enough to my darling friends for *their* generosity in coming out and giving of themselves for the sake of our Library."

The "talent," to whom Anne had been talking in the intervals, came and seated themselves in the front row and, very informally but with a touch of the theatrical that lent glamour at once to their personalities and their appearance, Ada Howland introduced her "dear, dear friends."

The tall, gaunt man in frock coat and fine, but slightly frayed, linen went up on the platform, waited until one could hear a pin drop, and then enthralled them with Hamlet's soliloquy and a scene from *Romeo and Juliet*. A young

183

girl, with pointed face and dark, poetic eyes, leaped onto the stage and whirled into a dance that left her audience breathless before she subsided, like a graceful flower, in the center of her billowing skirts. A portly little man, with rubicund features and a shining bald head, slipped a banjo over his shoulder and plucked from it melodies that set peoples feet to beating on the grass while he sang in a full, sweet voice old ballads of the South. A magician sent the children off into frenzied laughter pulling coins from their ears and guinea pigs from their socks. That was supposed to be all. But the audience would not go.

They shouted and clapped and stamped and howled affectionately, insistently, "Ada! We want Ada Howland! Ada, please, please!"

And, at the last, Ada Howland ripped off her magnificent hat, tied her bright head in a black shawl, wrapped a black cloth around her large body, and became, for their intense enjoyment, an immigrant Irish woman telling a neighbor about her life in the new country.

They loved every minute of it.

"I never had such a fifty cents' worth in all my born days!" Anne heard them saying. "That tall fellow—they say he was with the Ben Greet players, whoever they were; but they must have been good!" . . . "My, it must be wonderful to have friends like that! How do you suppose Ada Howland stands it out here in a quiet little place like this?" . . . "Well, whatever it was she wanted to make for the Library, I'll bet she made it!"

And she had—more than made it.

"I hadn't any qualms about cajoling people into spending money," Ada Howland said at the end of the afternoon. "They can afford it, most of them . . . and they *did* have a good time. I would have gone out and held up the bank, anyhow, if that was the only way I could get money for my children's room." Her happy laugh rang over the green. "And, you see, I didn't have to; I haven't counted it yet—Mr. Holliwell is over there by the summerhouse muttering figures to himself—but I know I have more than enough to do everything I wanted for the children's room, and more besides. We shall have rugs and little tables and pretty curtains and pictures and books, books, books! That's where you come in, Anne. Make me out a list of all the loveliest books for children; and I swear I'll get them, if I have to give another party next year!"

Ada wanted Anne to stay over with her; but Anne pleaded a heavy schedule for the next day, and at last, laden with half a coconut cake, a pound of fudge, an apron for her mother and six pot holders for anybody who could use them, she got away.

When she got to the Library next morning, she was bursting with anecdotes of the amazing afternoon she had spent. The beautiful weather—Ada Howland's "luck"—was gone, and in its place was a steady, chilly drizzle. Helen and Gertrude crowded around, demanding details and firing questions at her; but Rilla sat a little apart.

"She gives me a pain in the neck," Helen burst out, casting a disgusted look at the droopy figure. "She's enough to spoil my appetite these days."

"Leave her alone; she won't come out of it till she gets word from her Dill," Gertrude said, "and there's nothing we can do about it. Go on, Anne. How many people do you think were there?"

Anne was full of her subject. Stories spilled out, one after the other, and she soon had them laughing hilariously. No one even knew that the telephone had rung until Rilla's piercing shriek cut through the air, stilling their laughter as if they had been stabbed. They wheeled together and saw Rilla slumped over the desk, the phone dangling by its cord.

Anne was the first to reach her. She caught the limp body against her, automatically replacing the phone. "Rilla— Rilla, don't! What is it?"

But they knew, all of them. Only one thing could affect Rilla like that.

"He's gone!" she whispered. Her blank eyes fastened on one after the other. "He's gone. I knew it would happen. I knew I'd never see him again."

The girls clustered around her, offering their mute and awkward sympathy. It was so hard to know what to say, because they knew that nothing they could say would give the slightest crumb of comfort to Rilla.

"I didn't ask much of life," Rilla sobbed. "Just to be happy with Dill. I wish I could die. What am I going to do?"

It was like a cry in the wilderness. Gertrude put out her hand. "After a while, Rilla, there's work."

Rilla lifted a ravaged face; they were shocked to see how drained and gaunt it was. She was suddenly old. "I hate this work!" she cried. "I hate it! I've told you that—I only wanted to marry Dill and keep house for us, and be happy with him. That's all I wanted, ever. And now he's gone, and it will never happen, and there's nothing for me. Nothing."

Anne thought, "It must be dreadful to feel that way. You'd be like a ship without a rudder."

When there was no purpose in life, there was no life. Only a kind of drab, futile existence. How more than fortunate she was that she had work—work that she liked, and that could fill her days! It swept over her in a wave. There had to be work at the core of living. When other things were taken away you still had work, something in which to lose yourself.

Perhaps Rilla was being childish, but she was being truthful too. Anne bent over her, words of sympathy choking in her throat. Poor, lost Rilla! She had lost Dill, her whole reason for happiness, and so she had lost herself.

Rilla did not come back to the Library, and they had no way of knowing whether she would ever come back. Her tragedy stayed with them, sobering them and lending a new gravity to their days. The work was heavier than ever because of her absence; but they did it cheerfully, in a kind of gratitude that this devastation had not happened to them.

Anne had an invitation from Sue Merrill to spend the week end with her at Claremont. "And about time, too," she had written in her usual breezy fashion. "I've practically forgotten what you look like. Bring all kinds of clothes; we're going to do something of everything. I have a perfectly swell time planned for us, if I do say so as shouldn't. You can't turn me down, because that would be doing *me* out of it; so telephone me pronto. I'll meet you at the bus with the last of our precious gas, and after that you can walk—unless we work on our friends."

It was tempting, but there was so much to do at the Library. . . .

"Don't be silly," Gertrude Bremmer said. "We're only open Saturday mornings anyhow, and it's a bit dull this time of the year. We can handle it . . . and you can do as much for us one of these days."

"If we're lucky enough to be invited anywhere," Helen Grant said, with a grin. "Have a whirl for me, will you? I'm beginning to feel like Mrs. Nose-to-the-Grindstone herself."

It didn't take much urging. In the back of Anne's mind all summer had been the tantalizing thought that someday she would get to Claremont. Now it had come, and she was wondering how it would affect her. She had to face it.

"Have you anything on your so-called mind?" Sue asked her affectionately, as soon as she had her in the car. "To do, I mean? Because if so, get it off your chest. I've left a free half-hour from eleven-thirty to twelve, and after that you're at my mercy."

"Well," said Anne a little hesitantly, now that the moment was here, "there really is, Sue, if it wouldn't be too much trouble."

"Name your poison," Sue said cheerfully.

"I'd like to visit the Library."

Sue turned and stared at her with a ludicrous expression. "Suffering catfish! If that isn't a fine example of a busman's holiday! You aren't serious, are you?"

"Yes, I am, Sue. I have a reason for wanting to go. You needn't come in if you don't want to. . . . I won't be long."

"I won't. I owe 'em eighteen cents." She settled back under the wheel. "Wake me up when you come out. And don't bring any books—I warn you there won't be time to read."

Anne thought, "Sue must have forgotten how much I wanted to come to work at Claremont."

188

Perhaps that was all the impression your most fervent hopes and desires had on other people. After all, how could they realize, from your carefully casual words, what it really meant to you? Sue was probably thinking now that Anne was just being conscientious about visiting the Library in another town.

It *was* a beautiful building! Anne admired it again, with renewed appreciation. The manicured lawns, the handsome white façade, the grilled doors. She stepped inside, waiting for her heart to constrict a little. This is where she might have been. This might have been her background, instead of Kenyon County. Sunlight fell in broad slanting bends from the high windows across the polished floor, touching to new radiance the handsome chairs and tables, picking out with brilliance the colors of the bindings across the room. She walked through the sunlight to the main desk. Orderly, efficient, beautifully appointed. . . .

"I'd like to speak to Miss Whitcomb, if she's in?"

The girl at the desk said, "Right here." She called back, "Sophie, someone to see you."

Anne hadn't seen the girl at the far end of the central stack. And, if she had seen her, she doubted if she would have recognized her at once. But it *was* Sophie. The strange part was, Anne realized, it was Sophie Whitcomb, not Mousey, who was coming forward.

"Anne!" she cried happily. Even her voice was different, though still Sophie's. "This is the grandest surprise! I've been thinking about you all summer."

"Thinking about me, but not writing to me," Anne teased her.

"The same goes for you," Sophie retorted gaily. "I had

to send out scouts to discover if you were still in the land of the living. Can you have lunch with me? I'm off at one."

"I'm staying with Sue Merrill, Sophie, and she has every minute planned. But I just had to pop in and find out how you—how you—"

Sophie smiled. "Don't I look it?"

"You do. Are you as happy as you look?"

It was amazing, really. Sophie was literally transformed. Her hair was still dun-colored and her features nondescript, but she had an air about her now . . . an air of conscious worth, of assurance, of—well, poise. She was sure of herself and her value. It made her over. Having a more modish hair-do and a touch of make-up helped, no doubt; and Anne noted that Sophie was distinctly unmouselike now in her choice of colors . . . she was wearing a skirt plaided in pastel blue and rose, and a soft rose blouse with a striking blue and gold ceramic cock on her shoulder.

"Come over here where we can talk a moment," Sophie said. Her eyes met Anne's. "Do you like the change?" she asked boldly.

Anne was honest. "Anybody would who loved you, Soph. You're—well, you're the way you ought to be now. You took off your shell. And you thought you were going to be so miserable here!"

"I know," Sophie acknowledged. "I died a thousand deaths at first. I wanted to hide all the time. But they wouldn't let me. Miss Kittredge put me at the front desk at once; you've no idea how I agonized. The first few mornings I vowed I wouldn't come back to work. But there was so much to do, and people kept asking me questions about books, and what I thought, and could I get this for

190

them, and telling me things that I sort of—well, sort of forgot myself. I had to answer, and I found while I was answering I wasn't so miserable. It was only in between times."

Anne nodded sympathetically, afraid that by speaking she would interrupt this unaccustomed flow.

"Then after a while the girls more or less took me in hand . . . not exactly by words but by example. They all looked so pretty and springlike I began to feel out of it in my dull things. I felt I wasn't doing justice to them or my surroundings, and I tried out a little color here and there and they were so encouraging, so flattering, that I fell for it. . . . Besides," she added naïvely, "I really enjoyed it. And having color on did something to my spirit. And, having a different spirit, *I* began to be different. Oh"—she flung out her hands—"it's silly trying to describe it, but I suppose you can *see* the difference."

"It's wonderful," Anne said, squeezing Sophie's hand. "Don't you ever dare to be any other way after this, Soph."

"Don't let me burble on like a brook," Sophie said, with her new assurance. "Tell me about yourself. Are *you* happy? I can't—I can't quite make out."

Anne felt herself drawing up inside. This was the question she had been dreading all summer, that she had put away from her every time it had come up, that she was afraid to answer. But now she had to answer. Now she had to be honest—with herself and with Sophie. In a way, she saw, this was why she had wanted to come to the Library, because she knew that Sophie would put that question to her and she would have to answer.

A thousand things flashed through her mind in a swift

procession. It was as if she were seeing her summer, the past months, high-lighted like scenes on a stage. They were passing in review and she was not part of them, but a spectator. She saw the Kenyon County Library and her own ragged disappointment that first morning; Miss Nichols and the girls; the crowded workrooms, the more crowded stacks. She saw herself driving the Bookmobile, rebellious and hot and tired, over macadamed highways and bumpy country roads and dusty lanes . . . schoolhouses and groceries and gas stations, small private homes and remodeled stores and blacksmith shops and little halls . . . all the odd station libraries she had come to know so well. The hundreds of people she had met, sometimes unwillingly, sometimes resentfully, sometimes with curiosity, sometimes with interest. The old ladies and the young girls, the eager boys and backward children; the farmers and shopkeepers and village aristocracy and small townspeople and owners of rolling estates. The bits of their lives she had come to know; the way her own life had become involved with some of them.

She saw Charlie and Berta and Willem Harmsma and old Mrs. Anstruther. She saw Carrie Newton and Nina and Mrs. Twining and Kathleen Marple and Cissy O'Connell and Matt English. She saw factories and old homes crammed with antiques and little boxlike houses where happy families crowded; run-down farms and acres spreading opulently in the sun. Willow trees and brooks and flower beds and straggly fences crowned with rambler roses and tumbledown shacks and neglected yards and broken walls. Wealth and poverty; sickness and health; ignorance and knowledge; strife and peace. Old and young looking to her for adventure and escape and surcease and new horizons and strength and romance and inspiration. She had been seeing a cross section of life. Only Kenyon County, one of the lesser counties of New Jersey, but a cross section of life all the same. Vital and disturbing. Challenging.

The pictures faded and Sophie's face swam into focus again. Sophie was waiting, a puzzled little look on her face.

Anne said with a rush, "I've had the most marvelous summer, Soph, I don't know how I'll ever be able to tell you about it."

Sophie said, still puzzled, "Do you mean it, Anne? I thought, you know . . . at first you were so—"

"Disappointed," Anne grinned. "A mild word, that. Furious. Hurt. I just didn't know what was in store for me. Even after I found how much I was getting out of it, I refused to admit it. A kind of stubbornness, perhaps. I hated to admit that Miss Pruitt knew her stuff. Remember? She told me that I'd get as much out of it as I put into it. And after I put some of myself into it—" She caught Sophie around the waist in an impulsive gesture. "Oh, Soph, I don't see how you could possibly have had as interesting a time as I've had!"

CHAPTER FOURTEEN

THE DAY THAT JESSICA NICHOLS WAS TO COME HOME from the hospital the staff closed Kenyon County Library an hour early.

"It's never been done before, and it probably never will be again," Gertrude Bremmer said, "but this is an occasion."

They went together to her home, laden with a mountainous cake and a container of ice cream and boxes of flowers. Jessica was thinner, and somewhat paler from her long confinement; but her spirit was as gay as ever, and she threatened to do a dance on her crutches out of sheer joy.

"To think that I don't have to stare at those Venetian blinds any more!" she cried. "It's become a phobia with me —I'll never have one in the house. And I'm going to start a campaign to have motion pictures on hospital walls. And a private orchestra for every floor. And a committee to arrange a surprise a day for the long-term patients. It's the tedium that gets you—not the illness. I'll never complain again about being so busy I could drop in my tracks. Not after three months on my back."

She had been kept in almost daily touch with things at the Library; but, even so, there were matters that waited for her decision, and they had all had numerous opportunities to realize just how much Jessica Nichols' judgment and tact and business acumen had had to do with the smooth running of the Library. But she would take no credit for that.

"Nobody's indispensable," she said. "Most of us need an accident like this to make us realize it. You girls have carried on the work in a way to make me proud of you. My main satisfaction is in having trained you well enough to make it possible for you to take over."

"We'd never have got along at all without Anne," Gertrude said generously.

"Nonsense!" Anne protested, flushing. "I was the greenest of green, and I must have been a thorn in your side plenty of times."

"We couldn't have kept up the Bookmobile service without you," Helen said. "And, after all, that's a great part of the Library."

"One of you could have learned to drive," Anne said. "It doesn't take a giant intellect."

"Don't go modest on us," Gertrude teased. "We all know you were our sustaining limb, and the nice part is we like you anyhow!"

The party was a great success; the cake disappeared, and the ice cream. And they had laughed together about little amusing occurrences that they had saved up to tell Jessica.

"Now," said Helen, "we'll prove ourselves the perfect guests, and clear away the dishes. We won't have your mother doing it after we leave."

They began gathering up plates and spoons. "You're dears," Jessica Nichols said warmly. "But would you and Gertrude mind very much doing them alone? I want to have a little talk with Anne before she goes." When they were alone, Jessica Nichols put out her hand. "Sit down here," she said, patting a place on the chaise longue. She looked steadily at Anne a moment before she went on. "I suppose you've often wondered at my attitude," she said then, "when you'd come to see me and report. Listening, but not saying much. Not making any suggestions. Not asking many questions."

Anne nodded. "I couldn't help thinking—"

"It was hard on you. But it was a kind of test. I suppose you realized that after a while. . . . And don't think, Anne, that I wasn't fully aware of what a spot you were in. Or what a hard summer you were having."

Anne was a little startled. She knew Miss Nichols was astute and knowledgeable. But had she given herself away so completely? Miss Nichols answered her unspoken thought with her next words.

She smiled a quick, sympathetic smile. "You were very transparent at first, my dear. And don't feel badly about it. It was the most natural thing in the world. I knew exactly how you felt, and I sympathized with you. You were disappointed and hurt; you thought you were being put upon, that Miss Pruitt had been unfair and you deserved a better assignment than Kenyon County. Didn't you?"

Anne managed a grin. "My face gave me away apparently."

"More than your face. Your attitude. But if I'd shown you that I felt for you, it would have been your undoing. You had to work it out for yourself. I couldn't sell the Library and the service to you . . . that had to come from you. I wasn't going to influence you by so much as a word. And then I fell downstairs and bowed myself neatly out of the picture. You had to take on work you never expected to take on. Anne"—she squeezed her hand—"you'll never know how I practically held my breath, waiting to see how —big you were. Whether you'd measure up. Whether you had in you the stuff that I was hoping you had in you."

"It took a long time for me to get over my 'mad,' didn't it?" Anne inquired humorously. "I must be a stubborn sort of person. Long after I really wanted to, I wouldn't give in."

"But now——"

It was queer. Ever since that visit to Claremont, Anne had felt as if a weight were lifted from her. She had been laboring under it all summer; it had become a familiar burden. Not until she had been forced to reply squarely to Sophie's direct question had she known how much of the weight had gradually disappeared. And with her answer the last of it was gone.

"And now," she said, "I'm a changed woman."

"What changed you?" Miss Nichols asked.

"Oh"—Anne flung out her free hand—"so many things. I fell a victim to the surroundings, the atmosphere, the people I met. . . . After a time I simply couldn't hold out. So behold a convert!"

"Do you mean"—Miss Nichols spoke as if she were choosing her words with unwonted care—"that you might like to come back and be a part of Kenyon County Library after you graduate?"

Anne's eyes widened, and her pulse beat with excitement. "Do *you* mean," she returned, "that you'd really like to have me?"

She studied Jessica Nichols' face. There was only approbation there and, strangely, a kind of wistful expectancy. "You're a real find," she said, with her sweet smile, "and I've written Miss Pruitt so."

Miss Pruitt would have a right to gloat. But Miss Pruitt wouldn't. Anne gave her her due. She wasn't the kind to gloat. She had simply been a very knowing woman . . . knowing what was best for Anne, and Mousey—far better than they did.

She thought, in a rush of gratitude, "I'll have to go and make handsome apologies to her . . . not in so many words, of course; but telling her about my summer and how I feel about going back will be the same thing."

There were only two weeks left before fall term began. She had promised to stay on until the last possible moment so that Rilla's place and her own could be filled, at least temporarily.

"Rilla will be back, in time," Jessica Nichols said confidently. "She'll never make a good worker because her heart isn't in it; but I would take her back, just because she needs it so much. Maybe she'll grow, maybe not . . . but we have to give her the chance."

They were busy weeks; last-minute clearing up, last-minute cataloguing of new fall books, half a dozen last trips with the Bookmobile. Each one was like a good-by and a promise to come again.

At Gansville she found Carrie Newton in a familiar dither. The hall had been decorated and furnished; chairs had been installed, windows washed, and everything made in readiness for its first functioning as a community gathering place.

"If you want a thing hard enough," Carrie Newton said, "you get it. But I never thought it would take a fire at Grange Hall to bring this to pass."

Anne had promised to spend the night at Elmway and

go with Matt to hear Senator Phillips. Every ticket for the occasion had been sold—Miss Newton alone had done a heroic job, practically forcing each person who came into her library to buy a ticket as a patriotic duty—and then, two days before the great event, Matt telephoned her.

"It's all off," he said. "We're running in bad luck."

"What happened?" Anne cried. "Don't tell me the community hall burned!"

"Thank heavens, no. But it's just about as bad. The place sold out, everybody on tiptoe and expecting a rousing good evening for his money, and Senator Phillips' secretary sends word he's down with laryngitis and can't make it. . . . But, listen. You'll come out anyhow, won't you? Mother and I are counting on it."

"Oh, Matt, that's too bad! I'm so sorry!"

"You mean you can't come?"

It was pleasant to hear the disappointment in his voice.

"No, I meant about the Senator. What are you going to do?"

"Try and reach those we can, I guess, and refund their money. Refund the rest at the door, and hope everybody doesn't turn on us. What else *can* we do?"

It came to Anne in a flash of inspiration. She said excitedly, "Have a program, anyhow!"

He said, "Don't suggest another talk on soil bacteria. I've shot my arrow into the air for this season."

"No, no, don't ask me now. But if I promise to get together some grand entertainment for you, will you take me on faith? Do you think people would be willing to come and just have a good time instead of hearing Phillips?"

"What a question!" he mocked. "So long as they get their

dollar's worth I don't suppose it will matter whether it's Phillips or Burns and Allen. What do you have up your sleeve?"

"Not too much at the moment. But I'll call you back as soon as I have anything definite, and I promise not to be too long about it."

"Go to it," he said. "The only way I can show my appreciation at the moment is to say, 'Reverse the charges.'"

She laughed. "'By now. I have to get busy and burn up the wires."

She didn't give herself time to think or marvel at her own audacity. She called Ada Howland.

"Ada, I want your help," she said at once. "For some people you don't know; but you'd love them if you knew them, and they're in a spot."

And she told her about the Grange, and Senator Phillips' defection.

"Do you suppose," she said, her breath coming a little faster in spite of herself, "that you could prevail on those wonderful friends of yours to give us a program? The way they did for you? We could pay their expenses, of course, and a small sum besides." (She was taking that on her own responsibility; after all, the Grange committee would see the justice of it.) "But, of course, it wouldn't begin to compensate them for their time and energy. It's just—it's just—"

"Darling, of course!" Ada Howland's rich reassuring voice came back. "I know precisely what a pickle you're in. And they'd love to do it for you. *But* . . ." she paused dramatically, and Anne's heart sank.

She might have known the idea was too good to come to fruition. "But?" she repeated, questioningly.

"They've gone to the four winds, darling. Mr. Banning joined a stock company—I *do* hope it comes right for him, poor dear. He's had such a hard time; no one seems to need older actors just now. And Frank, the banjoist, you know, has had the most marvelous offer to do a spot at the Beaucaire; they're mad about his songs. And Leila, the sweet little dancer, has gone to try her fortune in Hollywood. I only *hope* she has enough money to see her through; but she was so eager I couldn't put a straw in her way, and she would have gone anyhow. And the magician—well, you wouldn't want a whole evening of a magician . . . and, besides, I think he's going out on a circuit, if he's not already gone. So you see—"

It had been ridiculous, of course, to think that just because you had an idea it could happen. But Anne felt as if she were a sadly deflated balloon.

"But"—Ada's voice, something about it, magically buoyed her up again—"but what about me? Would I do?"

"Would you do?" Anne fairly shrieked. "Would you really?"

"I'd adore it," Ada said. "I was just like an old battle horse that day, and now that I've got the scent of it in my nostrils I won't be happy till I have another whiff." She bubbled over with exuberance, with assurance. Her plans formed as she talked. "I think they'd like the Irishwoman sketch; everyone always did. And I do a nice French one, quite different. Oh, that makes me think— Why not a program of various nationalities? Say, five. Irish, French, Italian, American, and something else—I'll decide later. *If* you like that idea, of course."

"I do," Anne breathed gratefully.

"That would give them plenty of variety; if they didn't

like one they might the others. And you ought to have a little music in between, to cover my changes. What time would you want me to be there? And will you be sure to have a place for me to dress—just a *corner*, dear, but with good light and a mirror? And where shall I spend the night?"

"Don't worry about *that*! I'll fix everything," Anne promised blithely.

But it was more of a problem than she anticipated. There wasn't room at Elmway, and she didn't want to impose further on Mrs. English's hospitality. There was no inn at Gansville; the nearest one was at Fielding, and she knew nothing about it.

Carrie Newton solved the question. "*I* shall have her," she announced. Her voice was firm and surprisingly loud; but her eyelids batted in excitement, and the tip of her nose twitched. Apparently the words had amazed even herself. She added breathlessly, "Oh, Anne, may I?"

"It wouldn't be too much trouble?"

"Trouble! It—why, it would be the most wonderful thing that ever happened to me! An actress . . . Ada Howland, of all people, in my house. It would be something to dream about for years afterward. I used to see her in New York—oh, not more than three or four times; I never had much money to go in, you see. But I always loved the theater, and she was wonderful. I used to think, 'If I could be like Ada Howland, even for a day, I'd die happy.' And to think she might come and stay with me!"

"It's settled, then," Anne said.

She had a quick mental picture of the ebullient Ada and timid, fluttery little Carrie together. But it would work out.

Ada was kind; Carrie was adoring . . . and they both loved children and libraries.

The night of the performance was clear and starlit; and people streamed into the little Community Hall by dozens, crowding it to the very walls, exclaiming over the decorations, which had really transformed the place, and settling into their seats with pleasant anticipation.

"If you ask me," Anne whispered to Matt, "they're more relieved than grieved, not to hear Senator Phillips. But don't tell him so."

Matt had been very ingenious about rigging up a dressing room for Ada; he had also been appointed property man and general factotum. Anne was here, there, and everywhere, and the Grange ladies' committee simply gave up and handed over the reins to her. Promptly at eight-fifteen Judge Whitaker rose and a hush fell over the assemblage. People stationed along the walls turned out the side lights, Matt adjusted the spotlight, and Ada came on.

Ada "wowed" them from the start. Her magnetic personality drew them to her from the moment she stepped forward, her voice enthralled them, and her acting opened their eyes to the magic of the stage. Anne felt sorry for the accordionist she had engaged to play between scenes. Voices drowned out his playing, and they were frankly impatient for the intervening time to be filled so that their darling could come and hold them in the hollow of her hand again.

At the end, hushing their tumultuous applause, Ada said, "You've given me one of the happiest evenings of my life. Will you please let me come again sometime?"

Her smile encompassed them, yet each one felt as if the eager question were directed solely at him. Anne was reminded of that unforced surge of children's voices answering Peter Pan when these eager older people cried, with one voice, "Yes, yes!"

And Mrs. Samuels pulled Anne aside and murmured in an awe-stricken voice, "Do you really suppose she really meant it? Gosh, if she would, I bet I could sell out the house at *two* dollars!"

It was a gala evening. Ada, resplendent in blue satin with cascading lace and a new assortment of startling jewelry, held court in the center of the cleared hall, until finally Carrie Newton, hovering about like a mother hen with a precious chick, insisted that she must "come home now and rest."

Anne said, catching both Ada's hands, "I don't know how I shall ever, ever thank you."

And Ada answered simply, "My dear, if we don't help each other, what are we *here* for?"

Anne slumped a little beside Matt in the station wagon. She stretched out her feet and laid her head back against the cushion. "Don't call me till eleven, Jeeves," she murmured.

"Tired?" he asked solicitously.

"A little," she admitted. "After all, it's been quite a day; not to mention evening."

"You were a brick, Anne, to do this for me," he said warmly. "To do this for us," he corrected.

"It was fun," she said. "I enjoyed it."

"Tomorrow I hope the tiredness will be gone and only the satisfaction of having done a grand job will be left."

She turned to face him in the darkness. "It's funny," she said. "I need that sort of satisfaction less and less."

"How do you mean?" he said.

She knew that he must know, instinctively, what she wanted to say; but he was asking her because he knew, too, that she felt the need to say it aloud.

"You remember that lecture you gave me the first time we met?"

He nodded. "You've forgiven me by this time, I hope? I was a pretty brash fellow. I don't know what got into me."

"I needed it," she said. "It made me mad, but I needed it terribly. You saw I wasn't keen about the work I was doing. You said, 'If you make up your mind ahead of time too much you miss a lot; but if you go at it with a high heart, ready to enjoy whatever comes—' I wouldn't let you finish; I was furious to have a thing like that said to me. Because it was true. And I didn't want it to be true—for county library work."

She paused so long that he said gently, "And then?"

"And then I had it proved to me, over and over again, as the summer went on. Against my will. Against my determination not to let it be true. It was too big for me. Or, rather, the work, the people I met, the things I had to do . . . rolled together into something that was too big for me. I had to go down under it."

He said, "That's a cute little trick life has. It can be lots of fun if you take it as it comes."

"With a high heart," she inserted. "I found that out. . . . Looking back, I don't know just when I began to change; I really didn't want to know, I suppose. But it was happening. And now, lately, I've gone out each day, gone out on each trip, with a sort of—well, a sort of sense of adventure. Wondering what was going to happen, whom I'd meet, what new set of circumstances I'd run into, how I'd react. It got to be more than work; it got to be fun too. I don't know now where one stops and the other begins. I can hardly wait to get back next year."

He said quietly, "Then you're coming back? I thought you would."

"You had more faith in me, then, than I had," she returned. "But now the promise of coming back, getting into the work again, is like a reward being held out to me. There's so much unfinished business too. I've *got* to see certain things through."

"Such as—" he encouraged.

"Oh, getting Berta in to a doctor. . . . I *know* there's someone who could help her. Watching over Cissy a little, so that she isn't overwhelmed by Mrs. Twining. Seeing if I can't get Mrs. Twining to do something for Mrs. Anstruther. Working on Willem Harmsma so that he'll get a Seeing Eye Dog and give up his queer hermit's sort of life. Watching over the new little library stations that have been started, so that they don't die again for lack of encouragement. Trying to establish others . . . there are so *many* places where book stations are needed. Seeing if I—" She broke off and laughed a little shakily. "You see? It's really *got* me."

"If that's what my impolite remarks have done for you, I'm glad I made them," Matt said. She could feel that he was smiling in the dark. And then, quite suddenly, his voice changed; there was a deep, serious note in it. "D'you know, Anne, you're a pretty grand girl. Pretty. And grand. It's a winning combination."

She said lightly, "What am I supposed to say to that?"

"Nothing. Just let me talk. I've got a lot to get across. First of all, how glad I am that you'll be coming by this way next year, popping in, spending evenings with us. . . . When a chap finds a girl like you, he wants to see plenty of her. So that he can make her think as much of him as he does of her." Anne sat silent. "Are you home Sundays?" he asked abruptly.

She laughed. "It depends. But quite frequently. Why?"

"There's nothing to prevent my hopping a bus to your town, is there, on as many Sundays as you'll see me?"

"Nothing," she admitted, "unless it's your advancing years."

They turned in the long drive of Elmway; welcoming lights streamed from the low, friendly house.

Matt said, "Then expect to see me. There's so much for us to talk about, and to do—"

"With a high heart?" she asked gently.

He took her hand, held it close between his. "With a high heart," he promised. "And together."

3718